PRODUCING KNOWLEDGE, PROTECTING FORESTS

PRODUCING KNOWLEDGE, PROTECTING FORESTS

RURAL ENCOUNTERS WITH GENDER, ECOTOURISM, AND
INTERNATIONAL AID IN THE DOMINICAN REPUBLIC

Light Carruyo

THE PENNSYLVANIA STATE UNIVERSITY PRESS

UNIVERSITY PARK, PENNSYLVANIA

LIBRARY OF CONGRESS
CATALOGING-IN-PUBLICATION DATA

Carruyo, Light.
Producing knowledge, protecting forests : rural encounters with gender,
ecotourism, and international aid in the Dominican Republic / Light Carruyo.
p.   cm.
Includes bibliographical references and index.
ISBN 978-0-271-03325-9 (cloth : alk. paper)
1. Human ecology—Dominican Republic.
2. Conservation of natural resources—Dominican Republic.
3. Dominican Republic—Rural conditions.
4. Globalization.
I. Title.

GF527.D65C37 2007
304.2097293—dc22
2007031283

It is the policy of
The Pennsylvania State University Press
to use acid-free paper. This book is printed on Natures Natural, containing
50% post-consumer waste, and meets the minimum requirements of
American National Standard for Information Sciences—
Permanence of Paper for Printed Library Material,
ANSI Z39.48–1992.

The photographs in this book are
the author's own.

CONTENTS

ACKNOWLEDGMENTS

This book documents a small part of a lengthy and ongoing conversation with a long list of friends, mentors, and colleagues—from Santa Barbara to La Ciénaga—to whom and for whom I am deeply grateful.

Above all I wish to thank my family, especially my mom, Everis, and Uniit—there are no words; you are the absolute best. In the Dominican Republic, I wish to thank everyone at the Centro de Estudios de Género (CEG) at InTec, who so warmly welcomed me, sharing office space, insights, contacts, and the best potluck lunches ever! Thank you to Lucero Quiroga, not only for introducing me to the folks at CEG, but for many years of friendship—this book has benefited enormously from your insight and from your logistical support while I was in the DR. Thank you to both Denise Paiewonsky and Lourdes Contreras, the two directors during the time of this research. So many scholars and intellectuals in the DR (or close to the DR) took the time to talk through ideas with me and share their unique expertise—I would like to thank Angel Pichardo, Diane Rocheleau, Fatima Portorreal, Rayén Quiroga, Pedro Juan del Rosario, Elueterio Martínez, Rhadames and Yolanda Lora, Moisés Mendez, Edgar Cury, Arsenio Mera, Gail Mullen, Amy Shreck, Claudia Scholz, Ginetta Candelario, Alicia Sangro, and Didiana Belliard. I am truly in debt to Lilén Quiroga and Luís Toiraq, for without a long car trip and a lengthy conversation about dolphins, spirits, and empowerment, this project would not exist.

I was so fortunate to begin this work in the Department of Sociology at the University of California, Santa Barbara, under the direction of Kum-Kum Bhavanani and John Foran—my utmost respect and gratitude to you both; I could not have wished for anything more. There are many people to thank for many special reasons, above all, for so much rich and unpretentious intellectual exchange and emotional support (many of you have read and commented on the ideas presented here—you are not responsible for anything that you do not approve of within these pages): Lorena Torres, Lorena García, Vivian Barrera, Darcie Vandegrift, Peter Chua, Becky Overmyer-Velasquez, Elida Bautista, Helene Lee, Francesca Degiuli, Karl Bryant, Dana Collins, Molly Talcott, Christopher McCauley and Susana Peña (Susana, thanks for pushing me and for your excellent pep talks). Thanks must go to Avery Gordon for her wisdom, way with words, and great advice. Thanks to Jenny Sheffield and Barbara Harthorn for their help securing funding for the first stages of this project. At Vassar I have benefited from the support of a terrific group of people: Jennifer Ma, Laura Yow, Yvette Louis, and Bill Hoynes all deserve very special mention here, as does Katie Hite, who has been an exceptionally generous mentor and friend. Lisa Paravisini, Lisa Collins, Monique Segarra, Joe Nevins, and Dan Rourke each very generously read and commented on parts of this book. There have been many fruitful conversations with students at Vassar—particularly, I'd like to acknowledge Túlio Zille, Juliana Valente, and Ricardo Sanchez for the final-hour birthday brainstorm, and the students in my seminars Race, Nation, Gender in Latin America and Women, Culture, and Development (2004–2006). You have been such a joy to learn with and know.

My gratitude also goes to Sandy Thatcher, Christine Bose, and a second anonymous reviewer, who introduced me to the writings of some fantastic historians—thank you all for your feedback and I hope you notice its impact. Also thanks to Romaine Perin for her skillful copyediting and to Kristin Peterson at Penn State Press. Above all, I thank the residents of La Ciénaga and, especially, the women and men of Asociación Nueva Esperanza, who welcomed me, put up with my snooping and tagging along, forgave my slipups, and transformed my thinking. Thank you!

A 1999 dark-green sports utility vehicle (*jeepeta*) with tinted windows slows as it drives past. I am sitting on the ledge of Rita's porch, writing in my notebook, as I have done on many afternoons. Rita and her father are listening to the radio novela, and Miriam, Rita's eldest daughter, has just finished cleaning the house and is now polishing her nails. Francia sits with us while keeping an eye on the *colmado* (small general store) that she and her husband run next door and breastfeeding her baby girl, the youngest of five. A group of kids play ball in the dirt road in front of us; they attend school in the morning and have the afternoon free. Their play is interrupted by the dark-green jeepeta; a window comes down, and the driver, a middle-aged Dominican man wearing designer sunglasses, mumbles something to one of the kids, nods, rolls up the window, and drives toward the office of the park, located at the road's end. The kids run after the jeepeta for a few yards and then turn back to their game. Miriam blows on her freshly polished red nails and asks if I would like to paint mine. I do.

We are located in a community called Boca de los Ríos, the last stop before entering the national park—Parque Nacional José Armándo Bermúdez. This is the end of the road; it is the beginning of a mountain adventure for some, but for residents of La Ciénaga de Manabao it is a strategic location. It is strategic precisely because it is the end (of the winding mountain dirt road) and the beginning (of the park) and thus places the residents squarely in the path of visitors. "If it weren't for tourism we'd be dying of hunger," one man told me. Residents of Boca de los Ríos have an advantage over other locals. Their location means more access to tourism—obtaining jobs as guides, renting a bed or a room, selling from their colmados, renting out a mule, or benefiting from the "goodwill" of tourists. Boca de los Ríos is one of several communities, called *parajes,* or the smallest geopolitical administrative units, that make up

La Ciénaga de Manabao—its location makes these particular Cienagueros more highly visible than their neighbors.

I suppose what is *visible* depends on who the visitor is, and there are many.[1] Jeepetas drive in and out frequently enough to go unnoticed, except that nothing goes unnoticed in a small town. Here, a taken-for-granted skill is the ability to tell the difference between a motorcycle, a produce truck, and a passenger truck by their sound as they approach up the hill and, even more impressive to me, the ability to tell whose vehicle it is— "Oh! Here comes Kiko's truck!" The traffic in La Ciénaga includes tourists, politicians and military officers who have vacation homes or land in the area, people who would like to buy land, and the director of national parks and other park personnel. La Ciénaga is also visited by representatives from a variety of nongovernmental organizations (NGOs), environmentalists, and scientists from U.S. universities and their Dominican counterparts. Sometimes missionaries, supervisors from the coffee plantation up the road, and presidential candidates (by helicopter, of course) come to the area; even the vice president himself has visited, to attend a meeting of the local women's association, the Asociación Nueva Esperanza (ANE).

What visitors see might depend on the reason for their visit, where they came from, and their timing. An agronomist, or other person interested in agriculture, may notice that most of the small plots of land are being used to grow *tayota,* a squashlike vegetable. This was not always so; beans and coffee were much more common in the past and more profitable, I am told. Small farmers in the region can no longer compete with large agribusiness and imported beans. They lose money and accumulate debt, so most have turned their land over to tayota—which at least puts a little food on the table. Such an agronomist, if familiar with the area, may know or notice that some of the best land on the drive to La Ciénaga is owned by absentee urban landowners and is being used as grazing land.

Foreign tourists have commented on the amount of garbage seen on the side of the road, between houses, under small patches of coffee plants, or in ravines—shoes, batteries, plastic bottles. This garbage detracts from the beauty of the area, they say. *But there is nowhere to take the garbage, I say.* No sanitation truck comes to La Ciénaga, no recycling truck. And while

1. In an account that inspired me to think and write about how the journey to La Ciénaga is perceived, Michael Kustudia (1997) depicts his own contrasting narrative of arrival to the region. Jamaica Kincaid (1988) also plays with the poetics of what is visible to visitors in her critique of tourism and colonialism in Antigua.

residents have been asking for—and the Peace Corps was meant to build—landfills, nothing has been done. And just where does that tourist think the garbage she generated in the park and on her visit will be put, anyway?

When I rode up to La Ciénaga for the first time in May 1998, I sat in the back of a pickup truck with a history buff. As we drove past the pine trees and looked down the mountain into the river rushing below—a breathtaking view—he commented on the region's history. These are fairly new pine trees; these forests were all burned down by the military, he told me. Looking for guerrillas, he said. An artist might notice the colors and the architecture. The wooden houses that decorate the road are painted pink and green or orange and aqua, have zinc roofs, and are framed by trees and bright flowers of red, fuchsia, pink, and yellow. The faces of the inhabitants who peek out the doors and windows, or sweep patios, or carry water from the river ranged from black to very blond and blue-eyed. In La Ciénaga, where almost everyone is related, one woman told me, "Somos todos de las mismas familias, pero salimos de diferentes razas" (We are all from the same families, but we came out different races).

Perhaps there are some tourists who miss these important details as they focus on the river and imagine that in a few short minutes they will be slipping on their orange life jackets, slapping on some sunscreen, and hopping onto the raft that will take them down the river again. Or maybe they are focused on getting on a good strong mule and heading to the famous Pico Duarte or Valle del Tetero to escape the heat and traffic of the capital.

Clearly the eye of the beholder is of some consequence. Timing matters too, because had the driver of the 1999 dark-green jeepeta with tinted windows come to La Ciénaga in 1998, instead of on that particular sunny afternoon, he might have seen Clara come running down the hill with the yokes. She had marched herself up the hill through the rows of pine trees and removed the yokes from a team of oxen that were being used to transport illegally cut pine trees from her family's property. Had the driver rolled in a bit later in the afternoon, he would have seen Graciela selling coconut and potato sweets she made and sold so she could buy the evening's meal of fried eggs and boiled green bananas. In fact, it is possible he drove past Graciela on his way out, and maybe he even purchased a *dulce* for a peso. And a few days before he might have seen Junior wipe out on his motorcycle—show-off!

Had he driven in several months later, he might have seen Anita and her husband, eyes cast down, walking down the hill with a tiny bundle

and a shovel to the place where they would bury their child. She was born just before dawn, without enough warning to make it to the hospital (forty kilometers away), and she did not make it to sunset. Had he come on a Sunday, he would have seen people gathered together and maybe noticed fifteen-year-old Celina walking to the colmado just to flirt with Luis, the cute nineteen-year-old who drives the tayota truck to Santiago and always honks as he drives by on weekdays. But had he come two Septembers ago he would have had to turn around and go home, because Hurricane George destroyed the bridges and roads that lead to La Ciénaga, along with crops, homes, livestock, and schools. The bridge was no good anyway, but neither is the one in place now; some tourists even get out of their car and walk across, not trusting the rickety planks to hold up their heavy top-of-the-line 4x4, though one brave person does drive across. But it was on this particular day, and at this particular hour, that the driver of the 1999 dark-green jeepeta with tinted windows drove by, as we sat and wrote, talked, polished our nails, and listened to the novela.

The dark-green jeepeta signifies the presence of the tourist, the traveler, the outsider in whatever form he or she takes—ecotourist, researcher, missionary, organizer, or politician. Perhaps I imagine that the work I do as an ethnographer makes me different from the jeepeta driver, or the missionaries or whitewater rafters, but during my time in La Ciénaga, we were all tourists, travelers, outsiders. The account that follows is a combination of what was visible to me during the time I spent in La Ciénaga and what was shown to me by Cienaguera/os who were my hosts, guides, and mediators. I attempt to represent a tiny fragment of the lives and concerns of the people whom I came to know and care about while I was there. Although my visit was more than a cursory drive through town on my way to the park, and I adhered to most of the sociological conventions that would authorize me to write this book, I am certain that I cannot begin to do justice to the complexity of life in La Ciénaga.[2] Thus, this book can only be a story—a partial truth—that weaves together my own questions and anxieties about development with the voices that I encountered in La Ciénaga.[3]

Paradoxically, perhaps, I center local knowledge, while simultaneously questioning whether it is even possible for me to do so. I choose the local—

2. See the Appendix for a brief methodological discussion.
3. See Haraway 1988.

local knowledge specifically—as a site for analysis because I am interested in what it means and could mean to development studies. In a field in which the smallest unit of analysis is the capitalist world-system, the fact that Clara ran down the hill with a pair of stolen yokes, or that Celina may well run off with the tayota-truck driver, may seem insignificant. This is because development studies has not yet found a vocabulary to connect large structural processes to the ways in which people live, love, and labor. But the daily practices of women and men and the meaning they give to those practices show the ways in which they are not simply victims of development, but active participants creating, challenging, and negotiating the capitalist world-system on the ground. Therefore, an empirical study of local knowledge as dynamically constituted not only illuminates the relationship between culture and political economy, but also unsettles assumptions about the meaning of development and the workings of agency, thus opening up the possibilities for a more radical, informed, and potentially transformative dialogue.

LOCAL KNOWLEDGE

To get at this question of local knowledge, this book is framed by two questions: How have women and men in La Ciénaga come to know what they know about development and well-being? And how, based upon this knowledge, do they engage with development projects and work toward well-being? I am interested in these questions because I have been arguing for a development studies that more adequately addresses the relationship between large structural forces and people's lived experiences. Such a project must weave together and between historical narratives and ethnographic narratives, the voices of the author and the subject, silences and actions, global economies and local economies. I have chosen as my starting point local knowledge, which I argue is knowledge that emerges precisely from tensions between structural process and local lived practices and definitions of well-being. In other words, local knowledge is the way in which women and men make sense of the world and their own circumstances, and upon which they make decisions about how to create well-being in their lives and communities.

In the past couple of decades there have been a growing number of challenges to what have been exposed as the masculinist, modernist, and economistic assumptions that undergird development theory and practice (Sen and Grown 1987; Shiva 1991; Parpart and Marchant 1995; Escobar 1995; Vandegrift 1998; Chua, Bhavnani, and Foran 2000; Bergeron 2001; Freeman 2001). These critiques, which have come from multiple directions, have opened up questions about the foundational tenets of development, such as the notion that the West (particularly the United States) should be the model for all nations to emulate, and the importance of the first-world, or first-world-trained, development expert. Both of these were seen as key to overcoming the cultural constraints that were keeping poor nations poor.

Marxist development scholars, notably dependency and world-systems theorists, reframed the problem of "underdevelopment," exposing its roots in colonialism and in the very same international economic processes that created growth for the first world (Gunder Frank 1969; Cardoso and Faletto 1971; Wallerstein 1974). They avoided questions of culture entirely. More recently, scholars and activists have been concerned with the negative impact of policies intended to create national economic growth and development on communities, ecosystems, and local practices (Sen and Grown 1987; Shiva 1991). These studies have reintroduced an interest in culture and local knowledge, suggesting that these may move us away from universal solutions to problems that are unique in terms of history, culture, and geography.

Others have suggested that these "problems" of development are cultural constructs themselves. Arturo Escobar (1995), for instance, has rather convincingly argued that the third world and underdevelopment are the inventions of the first world—inventions that have been used since World War II to justify interventions made by the United States in the name of developmental assistance. And while he exposes the embeddedness of development discourses in first-world epistemologies and interests, one is left to wonder whether third-world actors—elite and non-elite—are more than empty receptacles into which first-world knowledge is deposited. Escobar himself implies that this is not the case by inviting scholars to produce ethnographies of popular practices, to encourage envisioning alternatives to development. Nevertheless, a marked tension remains between the overdetermining power of developmentalist discourse centered in the text, and the potential existence of "hybrid" place-based models to which he alludes (Escobar 1995, 96); this very tension opens up the space for new lines of inquiry into the making of local knowledges.[4]

Over all, critical discussions of development have been dominated by two troubling tendencies. One is the dismissal of local knowledge as colonized knowledge—merely reflective of centuries of colonial/imperial and debt domination by the first world and first-world epistemologies. The second tendency is the romanticization of local knowledge as the "authentic," "traditional," and thus automatically "counterhegemonic" opposite to first-world knowledge. These two tendencies are really two sides of the same coin. Without the presupposition of a "true knowledge," there can be no false knowledge. In this framework it is not necessary to *understand* local knowledge, only to center it or correct it. For instance, once folks remember that in centuries past, the organic agriculture used by their ancestors did not harm the land, they will willingly practice it. While this approach critiques modernization, it is entrenched in an enlightenment approach, which seeks to uncover an innocent Truth, as it is held by marginal subjects. This standpoint approach has been widely critiqued as it relates to the sciences in general, notably in the work of Donna Haraway (1988), Jane Flax (1992), and Stuart Hall (1992).

Parallel to, and often in dialogue with, these very critiques of enlightenment approaches to progress and development, we have seen in the past two decades the emergence of a plethora of theoretical and empirical studies that have taken on the development apparatus from a variety of

---

4. In later work, Escobar further develops his theoretical discussion of "local knowledge," particularly as it relates to place-based politics. He calls it "a mode of place-based consciousness (even if not place-bound or place-determined)" (see Escobar 2001, 153).

critical vantage points. While this is a vast literature, I would like to say a few quick words about two widely read and seminal works: Sen and Grown's *Development, Crisis, and Alternative Visions* (1987) and Arturo Escobar's *Encountering Development* (1995).

Sen and Grown's intervention combines structural analysis with analysis of the work lives of women to expose the ways in which economic development does not, in fact, benefit them. Sen and Grown ask development scholars and practitioners to center the voices of the most marginal populations of the world—poor third-world women—as a way of transforming the way in which development is conceptualized. Their contribution to understanding women and development by centering women's practices and suggesting a model of economics that centers women's well-being should not be understated. However, this approach been taken to task for not critiquing modernist assumptions about progress and for falling into a "cultural essentialism" that homogenizes and victimizes women (Mohanty 1991; Narayan 2000). In this model, culture and tradition remain things that should and can be overcome.

If Sen and Grown at their core maintained a modernist framework—in which the knowledge of poor women could expose a more liberatory development, and oppressive "traditional" cultures could be overcome— Escobar's *Encountering Development* (almost a decade later) was at its core a sharp and focused critique of this framework. For Escobar, culture cannot be overcome by development, because development, underdevelopment, and modernization's hailed "progress" are themselves cultural constructs. Specifically, he argues, they are first-world constructs that have been enabled by the relationship between knowledge and power—and used to legitimate a variety of U.S. interventions into the workings of "underdeveloped" states, economies, and peoples.

The authors of both these books conclude by suggesting a turn to the local. Sen and Grown call for a centering of poor women's voices as a way to envision *an alternative development.* Escobar calls for local ethnographies; by understanding local practices we may come closer to identifying *alternatives to development.* Each of these works provides an important critique of "expert" and "first-world knowledge" and sheds light on the workings of power in development theory and practice. And both share the assumption that local practices could lead us to alternatives. Likewise, I am convinced of the importance of the cacophony of voices that are marginalized—not because they are authentic or necessarily oppositional, but because, as

Haraway argues, a better science is at stake (1988), and, importantly, a more just world. If the real is constructed by a variety of interacting forces (Hall 1980), then it must also be that "accounts of the real depend on a power-charged social relation of conversation" (Haraway 1988, 593).

If it is both necessary and desirable to engage with something we might call "local knowledge," then it is first necessary to develop a theorized understanding of what local knowledge might be in the context of development studies. The arguments for local specificity that have been advanced by feminist development scholars (Harcourt 1994; Parpart 1995; Feldman and Welch 1995) should not be read to mean that the local exists outside or in opposition to knowledge that has been understood variously as "universal," "scientific," "first world," or "elite." When specificity is deployed as "cultural relativism," or read through a static understanding of culture, local understandings are dehistoricized and erroneously treated as if they could stand (innocently) outside the power/knowledge coupling that has created "universal," "scientific," or "first world" knowledge. Recent scholarship has also suggested that polarizing "local" and "global" or "Western" and "non-Western" in development studies precludes grasping the rich and complex interactions that occur in what Anna Tsing refers to as "friction"—those connections in which something new is inevitably created (Tsing 2005; see also Pigg 2005). Both Pigg and Tsing raise important questions about how to understand ideas such as *global, universal,* and *local* in more complex and dialogical ways.

Local knowledge should be understood as a logic that, like all knowledge, is situated; is constructed historically; and is fractured, fluid, and contested (Haraway 1988). To avoid making the false division between the local and the general/global/elite, local knowledge should be understood as always in dialogue with a variety of competing logics/knowledges that overlap and exert differing degrees of power—local knowledge is created and re-created in this dialogue. This dialogue interacts with lived experiences to shape analytical frameworks that both inform how meaning about well-being, development, and progress is made and provide the language with which subaltern voices enter into and engage with development.

This proposed understanding of local knowledge builds on Sen and Grown's centering of lived practices and well-being of third-world voices; on Escobar's deconstructive approach to development studies; and finally, to avoid false dualisms and integrate material and cultural analysis, on the theoretical contributions of British cultural studies—and those of Stuart

Hall in particular. Hall's work suggests that culture or, more specifically, cultural studies offers the tools to work through this seeming impasse between structure and agency. For Hall, and in this work, culture is defined as "*both* the meanings and values which arise amongst distinctive social groups and classes, on the basis of their given historical conditions and relationships, through which they 'handle' and respond to the conditions of existence; and as the lived traditions and practices through which those 'understandings' are expressed and in which they are embodied" (Hall 1981, 26). Thus, culture is understood as a process—fluid, constructed, complex, and contradictory, rather than static or homogenous. Culture, in this definition, is not only the reflection of an economic base, but also a site in which a variety of forces are expressed, challenged, and transformed. In other words, international interests, national development, local knowledge, and conservation are forces that shape one another, although perhaps to differing extents. It is the analysis of this dynamic interplay—and here Hall quotes Raymond Williams: "the interaction of all practices in and with one another"—that Hall refers to as "radical interactionism" (Williams, quoted in Hall 1981, 23).

By seeing local knowledge as created in and through culture, it is possible to see local knowledge and local processes as complex and part of the larger structures through which they are constituted and simultaneously constitute. Local knowledge is neither wholly created by the development discourse analyzed by Escobar nor stands outside it—indeed, serious work must be done on the role of local knowledge in creating and contesting the workings of development. The Woman, Culture, and Development (WCD) framework proposed by Bhavnani, Foran, and Kurian in their recent collection, *Feminist Futures* (2003), provides a lens through which such work on local knowledge can be done. The authors propose a platform for carrying out multilevel and dialectical analysis of development processes, avoiding the pitfalls of economic determinism and victimization of local subjects, particularly women. They do this "by putting women at the center, culture on par with political economy, and keep[ing] a focus on critical practices, pedagogies and movements for social justice" (2). As in the work of Tsing (2005) and Pigg (2005), such studies could recast the local not just as an authentic voice to be centered or a solution to be uncovered, but as a critical site in which to analyze the interplay of structure and culture. This reframing also demands new tools and a new politics with which to engage the multiple actors for whom development matters.

ORGANIZATION OF THE BOOK

In this book I suggest a way to think about this interplay between structure and culture by discussing the construction of "local knowledge" in La Ciénaga de Manabao, a rural community located in the buffer zone of José Armando Bermúdez National Park. Because of La Ciénaga's location, the livelihood of its residents is negotiated at the intersections of competing national and global imperatives—economic development and environmental conservation, agricultural production and ecotourism. On the basis of fourteen months of ethnographic fieldwork carried out between 1998 and 2001, in the following chapters I examine the multiple and complex ways in which development and well-being are understood and how they take form in the context of these forces.

In Chapter 1, I provide an historical overview of the relationship between national development and the lived practices of the Dominican peasantry. I highlight the tension that has existed between the creation of a "productive peasantry" as the vehicle for national economic development and the relatively autonomous practices that peasants carved out for themselves. Historically, as many women and men created rural livelihoods on the fringes of capitalist production, the government attempted to integrate them into national development and nation-building strategies through invitation (for instance, through land grants), coercion, and at times brutal repression. These strategies were meant to transform peasant autonomous subsistence practices—the way in which peasants achieved well-being— into sedentary and productive agricultural practices. Of key significance to the larger work is the fact that peasant knowledge has been created through these encounters and yet, at each turn, peasants have sought ways to elude the process of incorporation. While they have had varying degrees of success, this struggle nevertheless leaves clear indications that the development landscape has always been contested.

Refusal of and resistance to capitalist production has been and continues to be read as "peasant indolence." Because La Ciénaga is distinctly marked by its geographic location—defined by both the forest and the Cuenca Alta del Yaque watershed—conservation and development interests have been intricately interwoven. The watershed and the river Yaque del Norte are of critical importance to the country's agricultural lowlands and, as such, began piquing the conservation anxieties of the agricultural elite in the 1920s. Simultaneously, the rich forests have been of interest to the timber industry; in fact, it was this industry that in the early 1930s and 1940s stimulated migration into the otherwise sparsely populated area. However, deforestation caused by the timber industry has primarily been elided by discourses of conservation in the Dominican Republic, which have instead cast peasant practices as the primary threat to the environment. Thus, not only were peasants to be rescued from their "indolent ways," but nature itself—and, by extension, elite interests—was to be rescued from the peasants as well.

The strategies for rescuing nature from the peasants, and the peasants from their "indolent ways," have moved between mandatory production laws, strict militarized protection of forests, relocation of peasants, and most recently the fostering of conservation projects, particularly those revolving around the park and ecotourism. Tourism has been constructed as the solution to environmental concerns and poverty in the area. The lack of possibilities for and interest in relocation, the lack of markets for agricultural products, the presence of conservation funds, a reliable though temporal stream of tourists, and the history of criminalization of subsistence practices all lend a degree of credibility to the logic of tourism as the solution. In Chapter 2, I show the gendered ways in which ecotourism is understood and gained access to by residents of La Ciénaga. In particular, I reveal how and why well-being is secured not in a formal, or even informal, tourist economy, but through what one Cienaguero referred to as *enlace*—and what I call *gendered tourist-patron networks*—the ties that have developed between Cienaguera/os and tourists.

My focus in Chapter 3 is the seeming disjuncture between the narratives of absence or lack that characterize local representations of development in the area and the numerous interests and projects that are present. I analyze the context, development, and representation of two projects; the discourses surrounding development projects more generally; and the ways in which "lack" can be mobilized, with specific attention to the 2000 presidential elections. I argue that, as is the case with gendered tourist patronage, the *discourses of nothing* reflect points of analysis and strategy and reveal not only the making and complexity of local knowledge, but also the ambivalent relationship that locals have with development workers, politics and politicians, and researchers.

Local knowledge, as I argue, is not innocent; it partly holds together and perpetuates structures of inequality as well as resistance. In Chapter 4 I discuss the investment of local knowledge in "women's place" and "women's labor." While the "productive peasant" narrative was concerned with creating a white male peasant who was tied to the land (rather than a hunter or swidden farmer, which implied mobility), his counterpart, the "good woman" or "serious woman," was/is discursively tied to the home. Therefore, even while her (productive/reproductive) labor was relied upon, her good standing did not rely on productivity. It did rely, however, on her immobility (and, of course, by extension her reproductive work). In this chapter I discuss how women confront patriarchal notions of womanhood in their daily practices. While I look primarily at women who study, work, and organize, I do not center their workplace or their labor practices. Instead, I center *collisions of meaning*—the moments when differing meanings, expectations, and desires about women's mobility confront one another. Together these chapters tell a story about development in the Dominican Republic and specifically about ways in which women and men in La Ciénaga engage with development, create knowledge, and work toward well-being.

1

DEVELOPMENT AND THE CONSTRUCTION
OF THE PRODUCTIVE PEASANT

The lived practices and identities of rural women and men in the Dominican Republic's Cordillera Central, as well as the meaning they give to development today, is intimately tied to the history of development in the Dominican Republic. In this chapter I outline the key tensions between national development, which was predicated on the creation of a "productive peasantry," and the lived practices of Dominican peasants. This chapter is not a comprehensive history of the country; instead, I discuss several foundational moments during which these tensions can be clearly seen.

Throughout Dominican history, peasants have resisted and negotiated their incorporation into modernizing/development forces, and the development apparatus has found (and continues to find) new ways to incorporate them. Although this battle is not purely economic—in fact, as will be seen at different moments in time, it has been about land, production, race and identity, loyalty, order, repression, or freedom—it has been consistently couched in terms of peasant productivity, presumably achieved through the immobilization of the peasantry. The idea of immobilization emerges as key because it was the autonomy and mobility of the peasantry that posed a threat to production and, at times, to the established order. Therefore, the interventions I discuss are efforts to immobilize the peasantry in three overlapping ways: first, through the interruption of literal mobility, or the "sedentization" of the peasantry (Turits 1997); second, by immobilizing the peasantry within a class hierarchy (Pou 1987; Franco 1997); and third, by criminalizing peasants' shifting agriculture through environmental conservation measures (Rosario 1989; Kustudia 1997).[1] Additionally, the productive-peasant construct was eventually mobilized, both materially and discursively, at the intersections of capitalism and racism (González 1993).[2] That is to say, whether or not the peasantry could be disciplined into production, at the very least, the fiction of such a peasant (white, male, and, by extension, productive) could be used to gain international support for the emerging nation.

THE MAKING OF AN AUTONOMOUS PEASANTRY

The Dominican Republic comprises the eastern two-thirds of Hispaniola, the island it shares with Haiti. In a period beginning in 1791 and ending in 1803, led by Toussaint L'Ouverture, the inhabitants of the western third of the island (then known as Saint Domingue) fought for and gained independence from France and abolished slavery. Following independence, efforts were made to unify the entire island under the name of Haiti, abolishing slavery on the entire island, declaring Santo Domingo independent from Spain, and protecting the island from persisting French and Spanish colonial aggression (Franco 1997; Cordero Michel 2000). However, Spanish Santo Domingo was quickly recovered by Spain, and slavery was reinstated, persisting until 1822, when, following Santo Domingo's declaration of independence from Spain (1821), Haitian president Jean-Pierre Boyer unified

1. It should be noted that though my references here are to Richard Turits's 1997 Ph.D. dissertation, he has since published *Foundations of Despotism* (Turits 2003).

2. While it is beyond the scope of this book to analyze the scholarly debates on Dominican historiography, it is only recently that dominant accounts have been challenged in mainstream publications by Dominican scholars. Cordero suggests that historical accounts, particularly of the relationship between the Dominican Republic and Haiti, have been clouded by racism and the reification of a "racial problem" as the defining characteristic of the relationship between the two nations (Cordero 2000, 125). Franklin Franco (1997) has also leveled critiques at the ideological writings of Dominican historians, especially for refusing to engage with the subtleties of class struggle, which a Marxian analysis would help to illuminate. Historian Pedro San Miguel (2005) offers some insight into the multiple, and often competing, ways in which the island of Hispaniola has been narrated by the national intelligentsia. There remains a significant amount of work to be done to understand the complex history of racialization in the Dominican Republic in its global and historical context.

the island under his rule. Remaining in office until 1844, Boyer once again abolished slavery in Santo Domingo and provided land for those willing to produce agriculture for subsistence and export (Turits 1997).

The end of slavery posed a potential threat to the sugar economy, the most significant source of revenue for the nation at the time. Boyer attempted to balance this problem with land reform measures meant to end plantation agriculture and *latifundios* (which generated a great deal of animosity from the landowning elite, including the Catholic Church) while benefiting formerly landless people who were willing to use their newly acquired land for small-scale productive agriculture for national consumption. Boyer met an interesting challenge. His attempt to make newly freed citizens and landless peasants (including marooned slaves and black citizens who had bought their freedom) into productive farmers was met with resistance. Many peasants did not desire the land on the terms and conditions on which it was offered (Turits 1997; Moya Pons 1997; Mariñez 1984). This was partly because prior to the official end to slavery, many free black and mulatto women and men had already carved out autonomous lives for themselves in remote areas to escape slave society (González 1993). Moreover, those who had been involved in market production preferred to continue producing timber (*caoba*) in the south, tobacco in the Cibao, and cattle in the east; Boyer, however, was prescribing cacao, cotton, and sugarcane (Moya Pons 1997).

Peasants, it seemed, enjoyed a relative autonomy, mobility, and access to land that was facilitated by the existing land tenure system, known as *terrenos comuneros*. While the name implies public or literally "communal lands," the terrenos comuneros were actually private property that was owned by groups of people who inherited or purchased shares. This system of shares meant that each shareholder would have access to diverse segments of the land—agricultural land, pasture, streams, forests, and so forth (Baud 1995; Turits 1997). In this system, peasant squatters were tolerated by the landowners, and peasants used the diverse lands for cultivating subsistence plots, hunting, and foraging. While the peasants had no legal rights to the land, they enjoyed relatively free access to it. They used the land to hunt (*montería*) and tend to subsistence plots known as *conucos* (Bonó 1968; González 1993; Turits 1997). Turits hypothesizes that the squatting was tolerated by the landowners—who did not support the island's unification under Boyer's rule—in part out of fear that the peasantry would turn against them should they find themselves without access to land for subsistence (Turits 1997). To keep the peasants appeased, they turned a blind eye to peasant subsistence activity. In this way, seemingly unfavorable land tenure arrangements provided peasants with the autonomy to forgo incorporation into a plantation economy or state-defined agriculture and retreat into their own subsistence economy (Mariñez 1984). The nation was forced to turn to international laborers to sustain its economy. Thus, as peasants moved farther into the highlands to live independently from *montería* and *conuquismo,* thousands of *braceros* from neighboring islands were recruited to work in the sugar industry (Mariñez 1984).

Since land tenure systems and the vast availability of land were to some extent favorable to peasant autonomy, free land did not prove to be a good incentive to become tied to market production. Therefore, new ways to incorporate the peasantry had to be developed. Peasant autonomous existence and subsistence economies were seen as vagrancy or, as Turits describes, "non-commercial, non-capitalist existence; namely the peasantry's typical patterns of hunting, foraging, fishing, open-range breeding, and swidden agriculture on unclaimed and other freely accessible lands" (1997, 85). Additionally, autonomous peasant practices (labeled "peasant indolence") would continue to be racialized and discursively linked to free blacks, who were accused of not wanting to work for the common good or national progress (González 1993). Thus, for dominant sectors that were negatively affected by Boyer's policies—for instance, landowning elites and the Catholic Church—"blackness" came to represent both the Haitian colonizer *and* the autonomous peasant who "refused" to support the national economy (San Miguel 2005). The goal in the Dominican Republic became not to create wage workers in order to achieve progress, as in other countries in Latin America, but to make the peasant farmers more productive. Stagnation and failure to provide national self-sufficiency was blamed on peasants (Turits 1997). Throughout Dominican history there were various and complicated reasons for the state to attempt to coerce the peasantry into the national economy. For Boyer it was, at least in part, a way to develop an alternative to a national economy that had been based on black slave labor and to gain support for a unified island under his rule. He hoped to end a system that was based on the exploitation of black labor and replace it with one that relied on small agricultural producers who *freely* contributed to the nation's development. This is worth highlighting because it challenges the economistic framework that has been used to explain development in Latin America. It also exposes an interesting problem: the ending of one exploitative and legally sanctioned system of racial subordination presented a potential threat to the relative freedoms of another marginal population on the island and attempted to restrict the mobility and autonomy of the newly emancipated population.

DEVELOPMENT AND NATIONAL IDENTITY

Following a twenty-two-year period of unification under Boyer's rule, the Dominican Republic declared itself independent. Upon doing so, in 1844, the republic struggled to achieve recognition as a nation and position itself in a world economy in which, as Torres-Saillant states, "the 'racial imagination' ha[d] long since taken a firm hold" (1998, 127). Their economy weak and fragmented, Dominican political leaders for the following half-century sought to annex themselves to a large foreign power (Betances 1995). By securing assistance and support from a larger nation, such as the United States or Spain, the governing elite hoped to integrate the Dominican Republic into the international economy and create the conditions for economic growth.

In 1861 Spain reannexed the Dominican Republic, a move that was followed by the four-year War of Restoration (1861–65) and independence from Spain once again. Immediately following independence, under the alternating leadership of Pedro Santana and Buenaventura Báez, the Dominican Republic once again sought annexation to a large foreign power. To this end, a series of laws were established to simultaneously attract foreign investors and modernize the Dominican peasantry (Baud 1995). Throughout the late nineteenth and early twentieth centuries, state policy benefited the large, mostly foreign-owned sugar plantations and was often detrimental to cattle ranchers, tobacco growers, and especially peasant smallholders.

In dealings with the United States, the race of Dominicans was of significant concern—to both Dominican and U.S. political and economic elites (Duany 1998; Torres-Saillant 1998). One way for the republic to help ensure the much-sought-after support of the United States was to create an image for itself as distinct from Haiti. Haiti's black revolutionary history and activity was constructed as a threat. The Dominican state played on first-world notions of Africa and African peoples as uncivilized (Said 1994; Fanon 1967; Mohanty 1991) to raise support for itself as a nation and simultaneously delegitimize Haiti through the demonization of blackness. Haiti was used as a foil to the presumably white, Spanish, and Catholic Dominican nation. As I will discuss further below, it was important to *create the image* of a productive (white) peasantry to gain international support, even if it was not a national reality. In addition to the discursive creation of a white Dominican nation, the national government, not unlike those in other parts of Latin America and the Caribbean, recruited white settlers to populate the island, once again offering large amounts of fertile land to white immigrant farmers. This recruitment continued through the end of the century, with a significant number of immigrants from the Canary Islands taking land in the Cibao region (Inoa 1999). The intent was that these settlers would also, by example, change the farming and living practices of the Dominican peasantry (González 1993).

The dictatorship of Ulises "Lilis" Heureaux (1882–99) marked the beginning of a central government in the Dominican Republic, and it was closely tied to, as well as financed by, the sugar economy in the southern and eastern regions of the island (Baud 1995; Betances 1995; Moya Pons 1997). Because of this close relationship between the state and the sugar exporters, a series of laws were passed that favored the sugar industry and cemented the rifts between the diverse sectors of production on the island. The practice of encouraging foreign investment by virtually giving land away continued through the turn of the century, and the government was aided by the United States, which ultimately paid the Dominican foreign debt and took control of customs. The United States, by then with great financial investments in the island and with interest in maintaining access to the Panama Canal via the Mona Passage, sent in military troops, in 1903 and 1904, to protect its interests.

U.S. OCCUPATION

By the turn of the century the sugar economy had developed economic and political power, and the United States had full control of the sugar industry. In 1916, when the United States found itself unable to secure its interests through elite Dominican factions, it established direct military rule. As the foreign-owned, state-backed, southern sugar industry, with its largely Haitian and Dutch Antillian laborers, came to represent that which was foreign, the small growers in the Cibao region were held up as quintessential Dominicans—a romanticized notion of the white male peasant, or *campesino*. As a national symbol the campesino offered a distinctly Dominican identity whose (constructed) whiteness stood in contrast to the identity of Haiti, and whose Dominicaness stood in contrast to the essence of the United States. As Safa (1998) has pointed out, the Hispanic Caribbean has drawn on strategies of whitening the population to gain support from the United States, using ideas about Spanish lineage and civilization to erase the existence of people of color on the islands.

Rural women, for the most part, are absent from discussions about both economic development and Dominican identity during this period. This absence is part of a larger absence of women in the representation of Dominican history in general (Paiewonsky 1993). However, it appears that, unlike in the case of men, as I discuss in Chapter 4, their status as "good peasants" was reliant not on their role as "producers," but on their reproductive role. "Good womanhood," vis-à-vis the nation, seems to have been based on standards of decency, propriety, and proximity to the private domain discursively attributed to, if not always embraced by, elite women (Martínez-Vergne 2005). Regardless of the tropes of "good womanhood," which were clearly connected to immobility (proximity to the home and protection from the public domain), the economy had long relied on the work of Dominican women, as they had been agricultural laborers and vendors during and since slavery (Albert 1993). In her study of women and work in the Dominican Republic between 1900 and 1950, María Angustias Guerrero (1991) documents evidence of women working as seamstresses in the garment industry, as well as in agricultural production, transport, and market activities (see also Pau et al. 1987). Rural women also migrated to urban areas and, according to municipal records of 1880–1916, were represented in wage work, including as domestic workers, merchants, sex workers, cooks, nurses, midwives, small shop owners, healers, and teachers (Martínez-Vergne 2005). Working-class women's lived reality was, by definition, at odds with the construction of "good womanhood" on which order and progress were predicated.

During the time of occupation by the United States (1916–24), the U.S. military regime promoted national development by carrying out public works, instituting internal revenue collection, creating a repressive national guard, and building a system of roads connecting previously isolated locations of the island (Moya Pons 1997). Additionally, there was a massive effort to modernize the peasantry through legislative measures, particularly property laws, agricultural and forestry measures, and legislation against vagrancy. The construction of the peasantry as innocent—noble but backward—created a space for development and modernizing discourses that proposed to bring technology, education, and civility to rural culture and economy. Alcohol consumption was also banned and "civilized" pastimes such as baseball were instituted (Baud 1995). The sugar industry represented an interesting paradox for Dominican identity: the white Dominican construct was used to attract foreign investment for development and modernization, but it simultaneously posed a threat to Dominicaness by virtue of both its ownership and its labor force. The (largely fictional) white male peasant was used as a symbol, coerced into modernization, and simultaneously displaced by the sugar economy.

If the peasantry was to be modernized, the ability of peasants to live autonomously would have to be undercut (Baud 1995), and subsistence based on shifting agriculture, foraging, and hunting would need to be replaced by that of the sedentary productive peasant. In 1920 the Ley Forestal (Forest Law) legislated against shifting agriculture and served to further restrict peasant access to land and autonomous subsistence (Baud 1995). The law was framed as protection for the forests, but as Baud points out, peasant farming accounted for only a fraction of the damage to forests that was being caused by the timber industry. The damage caused by the timber industry was, and continues to be, absent from most discussions of Dominican forests. Instead, the role of the peasantry has been highlighted, which has served to demonize the peasants' subsistence activities and daily practices (Kustudia 1997) as a means to immobilize them and thus incorporate them into capitalist development. Strategies of resistance to these laws to modernize the peasantry were varied. These strategies, which have received relatively little attention, included move-ment further into the cordillera; anti-imperialist religious movements, such as Palma Sola; and armed resistance, dismissed by many at the time as banditry (Mariñez 1984; Martínez 1990; San Miguel 1995).

TRUJILLO AND BEYOND

While the U.S. occupation ended in 1924, its legacy remained in the leadership of Rafael Trujillo (Moya Pons 1997; Roorda 1998). Trained by the United States Marine Corps, he aptly built on the tools of rule and repression that had been used by the United States during the years of the occupation (Moya Pons 1997; Roorda 1998). He used "violence, terror, torture, and murder" to secure domination over the Dominican populace (Moya Pons 1997). He was also quite skilled at negotiating consent and support; for instance, he used his vision for modernization and staunch anticommunism to gain U.S. backing (Roorda 1998), and he became a patron to the productive peasantry to win their support (Turits 1997).

For these reasons, Trujillo's dictatorship represented the most significant attempt to end peasant mobility and autonomy. As Turits points out: "The regime sought to transform various everyday practices in the name of 'progress' and 'modernity,' particularly ones related to work, hygiene, and education. As well as being 'sedentary' and 'productive,' the new Dominican peasant was to be 'sanitary' and literate'" (1997, 629). Trujillo is particularly important to this study not only because of the repressive and extreme ways in which he influenced lived practice and production for rural Dominicans, but also because the subjects of this study remember him well. Their experiences have grown out of the history of development in the nation; they have been most directly affected by the Trujillo regime. In addition to the antivagrancy laws, there were laws for mandatory education, latrines, appropriate attire, and so forth. Hard work was rewarded in the discourse of the era. Every man had to cultivate ten *tareas,* and Trujillo billed himself as a friend to the workingman, particularly the working peasant. Those men who did not comply with mandatory cultivation were jailed.

Land reform was also carried out by way of agrarian reform, whereby families were resettled in colonies as a way to both appease the peasants and increase agricultural production (Mariñez 1984). Additionally, these colonies were meant to populate remote areas with peasants and (white) immigrants who felt loyalty and indebtedness to Trujillo. Peasant colonies also served the purpose of constructing a white nation, or at least one that could be imagined as white. Spanish settlers were placed throughout the Cibao region.

The Trujillo era is also significant in the area of forestry. While the majority of the timber industry's activity was in the south of the island, the Cordillera Central was also tapped as a source of commercial forestry. Infrastructure begun during the U.S. occupation—roads and highways connecting the Cibao with the capital—aided the growth of the timber industry. In some parts of the Cordillera Central, including the area surrounding the Yaque watershed, roads were created specifically for the transport of timber (Kustudia 1997; Georges 1990). Many men and their families moved to these areas to work in the timber industry, and many of the older residents had their introduction into the wage labor economy. Corporate access to the trees was based on buying rights to the trees, not the land. The land remained legally in the hands of the state, while national (private and state-owned) and international industry made use of the trees. This, as Kustudia (1997) points out, meant that little care was taken to reforest or cut in sustainable ways. Histories of the forests, however, make little reference to the timber industry, choosing to focus instead on peasant "slash and burn" or swidden agriculture as the primary threat to the environment (see Chapter 2). In line with this focus, there were very harsh laws in place to protect the forest during this period. Peasants became the "enemies of the forest" (Martínez 1990; for a critique, see Rosario 1989).

There seems to have been an additional issue of the possibility of enemies "in" the forest. Although it has been difficult to locate written accounts of this, several leftists and intellectuals I interviewed connected the repressive control of the forests to state counterinsurgency carried out by the regimes of Trujillo and Joaquín Balaguer. In other words, underpopulated forest areas were prime hiding places for potential guerrilla activity and peasant organizing and, some believe, were thus burned down by the military or populated with regime-friendly colonists. The timing of widespread forest fires in the early 1960s does lend credibility to this theory. And certainly it was the case that the Cuban Revolution brought increased concern about the potential of rural subjects to act as agents of revolutions. This realization, in fact, triggered increased land reform throughout Latin America, especially following the meetings at Punta del Este in 1961 and the resulting Alliance for Progress (Gill 1997; Escobar 1995; Sanchez 1994). Jared Diamond (2005) reports "counterinsurgency" among the reasons given for Balaguer's "environmentalism" (specifically, the eviction of forest communities from protected lands), though he indicates that he did not find documented evidence to support the claims made by his interviewees.

It is the case that trees and the forest, especially during and following Trujillo's dictatorship, became "sites of struggle" (Rocheleau and Ross 1995) between the state and peasants. Peasants cut trees to demonstrate resistance to state repression (Rocheleau and Ross 1995), and the military threatened peasants' livelihood, often burning small farm plots and replanting them with pine trees. The Dominican peasantry continued to rely on shifting agricultural practices as a source of subsistence, and the government was in tune with the profits to be made with the timber industry (Georges 1990). I am not proposing that the peasantry lived in, and was thus defending, some type of harmonious symbiosis with the forest that was disrupted by the state. Instead, because the state was using trees as a tool for control over the peasantry—attempting to control their subsistence activities, their mobility, and quite possibly their political associations—the peasantry resisted these measures in ways that, as they themselves recognize, were often equally destructive.

POST-TRUJILLO TO THE PRESENT

Over the past thirty years, the country's rural population has decreased by 31 percent. The growth of the service economy, tourism, and free-trade zones has resulted in an increasingly urban population. Additionally, there have been mass migrations to the United States, both the mainland and Puerto Rico. The lack of access to farming lands, vigilantly enforced by the military, coupled with the decreasing markets for small farmers, has meant mass migrations for rural men and particularly women, who make up approximately 56 percent of the migrant population (Pineda 1990; Safa 1995a). The nation no longer relies on Dominican farmers for staples such as beans. Therefore, small farmers often incur great financial loss when attempting to grow food for consumption and the market. For campesinos, "hechar dia," or day labor, is the most viable way to subsist. This is especially true given the increasing numbers of landless men, as well as the fact that women have rarely controlled the income from agricultural production, though they have always participated in the labor. In areas of the Cordillera Central, where I conducted research for this book, much of the land that was once farmed by campesinos is now reforested. These pine forests stand as evidence of a time, twenty to thirty years ago, when many residents were forced by the military to stop farming and plant trees. Some were offered incentives such as eventual profits from the timber, agreements that, in the main, have not been honored. Other residents were forced to reforest by means of extreme measures, such as the troops themselves setting fires to local crops and planting pine trees in their place.

Different rural areas, or *campos,* in the south, east, and Cibao regions have different histories, some more tied to sugar, or tobacco, or timber. Manabao and beyond in the Cordillera Central region (also referred to as part of the Cibao), the area that is the subject of this study, has its own unique history and patterns of development. This region may have served as a shelter from wage work and land laws because of its remoteness. There were two significant and conflicting challenges to the remoteness of this area—timber interests and conservation interests. Drawn to the rich, and less monitored, forests of the Cordillera Central, the timber industry introduced residents to wage labor and set off a significant wave of migration to the area. The population more than doubled in the 1940s as a result of opportunities for paid labor in the timber industry (Kustudia 1997). Motivated by their interests in the Yaque watershed, a source of water for a significant part of the country's agricultural lowlands, conservationists had begun to make their appearance as early as the 1920s (Pérez Rancier 1972). What is somewhat puzzling is the lack of documented discussion of these two diametrically opposed forces. The silences seem to be a result, at least in part, of the fact that conservationists and the timber industry seemed to be drawn from the same group—elite Santiagueros who either owned land or had rights to logging the land in the area. The natural reserve created to protect the watershed—now a national park—is in some ways the culmination of the struggle between the two forces. However, the arguments for its creation, as expressed by early conservationist Juan Pérez Rancier (1972), were focused on rescuing nature not from the timber industry, but from peasants. As is to be expected, the creation of the park has very much affected the daily practices, economy, and sense making of residents of the area, limiting their mobility as farmers and restricting the ways in which they can use natural resources.

The forest reserve, now called José Armando Bermúdez National Park, became yet another way to undermine peasant mobility. Its boundaries serve to remind campesinos that they have reached the end of the line. However, development and the conceptualization of a "productive peasant" have changed. The market and the nation now rely on a highly mobile rural subject. There is no room in the market for the small farmer, who has been displaced by corporate agriculture and imported food products— even the staple foods are imported. Meanwhile, industrial free-trade zones,

beach resort tourism and other service industry work, as well as international migration offer rural women and men who migrate possibilities
for generating income. It is clear that women and men who chose to stay in
rural areas are faced with decreasing possibilities for well-being based on
market agriculture. In many places, international and national nongovernmental organizations (NGOs) have tried to take up the slack by implementing
projects designed to generate income and stimulate sustainable agricultural
production. It is now the task of the NGOs to fund and facilitate the "productive peasant" lifestyle for those women and men who do not migrate.
For the residents who remain in La Ciénaga, despite the tenuous relationship
they have had with the military and government over the uses of land
and trees, the park is a source of livelihood. This is true both because the
protected watershed draws funding from international conservation projects
and because the park draws tourists. It is to this relationship between the
park, the tourists, conservation interests, and the livelihood of Cienaguera/os
that I turn in Chapter 2. This relationship indicates the ways in which
campesinas and campesinos continue to define and restructure the terms
of their engagement with development.

2

ENCOUNTERS:
TOURISM, CONSERVATION, AND GENDERED
TOURIST PATRONAGE IN LA CIÉNAGA

In this chapter I examine how discourses of conservation have helped create a logic about the value of ecotourism as the most appropriate road to development in La Ciénaga. Both women and men in La Ciénaga hold tourism as the key to development in the area, despite the fact that tourism is a much more marginal part of the economy than agriculture and offers women few opportunities for direct access. Development workers who seek to carry out nontourist projects, such as agricultural, latrine, or literacy efforts, often complain that people in La Ciénaga do not participate, that they do not want to work, and that they want everything given to them for free. The data I collected indicate that residents both desire and work toward well-being. Additionally, the data suggest that there are three main reasons why tourism has become, in the minds and choices of Cienaguera/os, the foremost avenue to working toward well-being in La Ciénaga. The first is their historical relationship to conservation, which has criminalized local agricultural practices in order to "rescue" the Yaque watershed. The second is the decreasing possibility that small farmers can subsist on, or find a market for, the agricultural products they grow. And finally, the ecotourist economy, which has been promoted as the environmentally friendly alternative to agricultural production, has opened up a space in which community members can negotiate well-being by building relationships with tourists; I refer to this space as *gendered tourist-patron networks*.

PEOPLE IN LA CIÉNAGA DO NOT WANT TO WORK

In conversations with both Cienaguera/os and other people familiar with the area, I often heard it expressed that the problem with development in La Ciénaga was that the residents did not want to work. It is common to hear "Todo lo quieren da'o," or "Todo lo queremos da'o"—"they" or "we," depending on the speaker, wanted everything given to them.[1] However, in my interviews and participant observation, I found that women complained of having no opportunities for paid work and male growers complained of having no market for their food. Moreover, most people worked *a lot*. There were times in the off-season when male guides practically ran over one another to reach tourists who had arrived to climb to Pico Duarte, the former struggling to secure a two- or three-day position (trip) as the tourists' guide. Many men grew some tayota, even if it was on borrowed land. More than 150 men were guides. Only a handful had permanent positions as rangers; one worked for the hotel owner and another for high government official who owns a house in the area. Day labor was often unpaid and done as a favor for a relative or friend, often being compensated by some of the crop, during harvest season.

Women worked most of the day. In addition to performing daily household labor, rearing children, raising animals (especially chickens and pigs), and tending to their crops (especially coffee and tayota), a handful of women attended college; worked as day laborers, community organizers, or colmado (small general store) owners; worked in their husbands' colmados; made sweets and other snacks to sell; or engaged in a combination of these activities.

While the idea that residents do not want to work, but want everything *da'o,* does not accord with daily living in La Ciénaga, it does resonate with classical and neoclassical modernization notions of third-world "culture," characterizing it as what impedes "progress" in the third world (Lipset 1986; Rostow 1960). For instance, lack of agricultural productivity in the

---

1. *Da'o* is a contraction of *dado,* meaning "given."

country has been blamed on campesinos being ignorant, lazy, and lacking initiative (for a critique, see Dore Cabral 1986). And in the case of land reform debates, "campesino laziness" was used to justify the expropriation of their land for large agribusiness, which continues to be seen as the answer to agricultural production problems in the Dominican Republic (Dore Cabral 1986). Again, these discourses of modernization have histori- cally been used to justify a wealth of first-world and elite interventions into the lives of third-world people, attempting to integrate them, as I discuss in Chapter 1, into first-world markets and value systems by turning them into "productive peasants" (see also Escobar 1995).

Notwithstanding the fact that people in La Ciénaga both work and want to work, there is, in fact, a high level of reliance on *lo da'o,* presumed to be that which is not worked for, but received for free. This term is often used to refer to the material benefits secured by way of what, in dis- cussions of politics in Latin America and the Caribbean, are understood as patron-client relationships.[2] In La Ciénaga, lo da'o includes, but is not limited to, material goods received during election times or as incentives for party loyalty. And though I touch briefly on party politics in Chapter 3, my focus here is on the ways in which well-being is negotiated in rela- tion to middle- and upper-class tourists. If campesino "laziness" is not to be understood as the reason behind a reliance on lo da'o, how is it to be understood? Common approaches to understanding the third-world rural poor suggest that they are victims, beneficiaries, or tricky system abusers who use the system but fail to produce. I argue that none of the current paradigms for understanding campesino engagement with aid/assistance/charity, or, colloquially put, lo da'o, is adequate. There are clear-cut economic reasons to rely on assistance, such as the fact that no matter how much tayota a grower produces, he or she is still unlikely to be able to buy medicine or provide an education for his or her children. And it is clear that people worked, wanted to work, and even complained of having no work. What is at stake is what people considered *worthwhile* work. Local definitions of development and progress, as well as lived experiences, shaped this crucial notion, which often revolved around ecotourism.

2. Javier Auyero (1999, 2002) has shed light on the ways in which patron-broker-client relationships, when understood from the point of view of the "clients," reveal a great deal more than the simple buying of votes. In fact, he suggests that from this vantage point, a complex network of political accountability becomes visible.

TOURISM AND CONSERVATION

Tourism and conservation are interlinked processes that for almost a century have been attempts to make Cienaguera/os into agents of conservation and have shaped how they define development and progress. As early as the 1920s, there has been interest in the conservation of the Yaque watershed, mostly on the part of lowland agricultural elites, who depend on the river. Juan Pérez Rancier's memoirs contain a combination of journal entries and official reports written by Pérez Rancier and his colleague Miguel Canela Lázaro during their explorations of the Yaque watershed area in the early 1920s (Pérez Rancier 1972).[3] The now-mythical "Don Juan," as Pérez Rancier is referred to by locals, represents one of the first documented clashes between residents in La Ciénaga and the interests of the powerful oligarchies in other parts of the country, most notably Santiago. Pérez Rancier and Canela were concerned with conservation because "the disappearance of the forests is the cause of the disappearance of the sources of water that supplied towns and cities" (Pérez Rancier 1972, 113). Throughout their 1926 report to the secretary of agriculture and immigration, the causes and consequences of deforestation are outlined, and all references to water are italicized to highlight their importance as water sources *for urban centers* in the Cibao. The Cibao region was the most important agricultural region in the country, supplying the majority of products for national consumption, particularly consumption in the capital (Mariñez 1993). It was extensive, with rich land and diversified crops and, importantly, home to a powerful Dominican oligarchy and agricultural elite (Mariñez 1993).

The report indicates that the significance of the river Yaque del Norte to livelihood in places such as influential Santiago was grasped as early as 1910. The report also blames the handful of residents (ninety-five in total in 1926) for the rapid demise of the forest, citing such activities as slash-and-burn agriculture, fire, *montería,* and the search for wild honey as the fundamental threats to the water sources. Interestingly, there is no mention whatsoever of corporate logging, which had been affecting the region since the turn of the century (Martínez 1990; Dotzauer 1993). It is impor-tant to note that the major loggers in the area were also the elite families

---

3. Jared Diamond, in his latest book, *Collapse* (2005), makes brief mention of this expedition.

from Santiago. Nevertheless, it was the campesinos who were cast as the threat to nature and, by extension, to the livelihood of urban dwellers. In their argument to create a protected area and remove residents, the authors state: "The case of the Yaque del Norte is clear and precise. Half the nation lives off the Yaque. Should the interests of this large portion of the population be sacrificed to the misguided interests of half a dozen miserable souls that we will discuss below and that with no mercy whatsoever are destroying the very sources of this indispensable and legendary river?" (Pérez Rancier 1972, 117). Here area residents were not only dehumanized (miserable souls), but also pitted against the interests of the urban population and agricultural producers in the lower regions of the Cibao. The approximately one hundred residents (who had been driven into the Cordillera largely as a result of losing their lowland plots to large landholders and foreign sugar plantations, or because they were recruited to work for the logging industry), and the work they did to subsist, single-handedly became a threat to "half the nation." The land, the nation, and elite interests became their victims. At the same time, completely absent from the reports was the fact that the principal threat to the conservation of the water sources for elite Santiagueros was, in reality, the logging activities of elite Santiagueros themselves.

Why are the expeditions of Don Juan important to Cienaguera/o thinking about local knowledge? The discourses of "campesinos as threat"—and the rescue of the land, the nation, and elite interests that these discourses engendered—have not only informed policy making for decades, but also helped shape local knowledge about work, development, and progress in La Ciénaga. While the region suffered a great deal more deforestation at the hands of government and private logging in the 1940s and 1950s, conservation discourses have painted the local residents as responsible for damage to the forest area (Lynch 2006; Kustudia 1997). This has yielded a variety of measures, such as relocation of families, threats of relocating entire communities, increased surveillance of the region, establishment of a military post in the area, and state purchase of all the land surrounding the water sources to create a protected area. Many local subsistence practices have been prohibited—among them hunting, shifting agriculture, and extraction of plant matter from the park (including medicinal plants and fuel wood). Silvina, a Cienaguera in her early sixties, spoke of how reforestation occurred during the Balaguer regime in the 1970s: "[Foresta, the militarized forest service,] planted pine trees wherever they felt like it. Because you see all those pine trees planted there—all of those are planted on someone's property. Foresta did not buy land here to plant trees. They came in here and if you had a plot of yuca they would chop it down and plant pine trees right there inside the yuca. And that is why you see these hills planted with pines, but all of that land, all of it, has its owner." Silvina's account highlights the (often silenced) antagonism between peasants and conservation efforts. Conservation efforts quickly became another means by which to subvert peasant mobility, literally restricting and managing peasants' subsistence activities in ways that have ultimately made survival largely dependent on wage work. Not only did the national government "actively promote" reforestation with the help of Foresta, but it also completely eliminated residents' access to trees; absolutely no tree, in or outside the park area, can be cut without permission from the government. Failure to comply with these measures leads to harsh punishments. For these reasons, among others, it is common to hear people say that the forest and campesinos are "enemies."

For Cienaguera/os, Don Juan was an explorer. In one interview I conducted, his encounter with the park was even called *la conquista* (the conquest). Quite an apt metaphor, given that his arrival implied radical changes for those who lived off land that became protected at his recommendation. And in the telling of the history of the park, he is also invoked as "the man who made the reserve" (el que hizo el vedado). The language of conservation present in the Pérez Rancier documents is also present in talk in La Ciénaga today. For instance, one older male resident told me proudly: "Everyone depends on this water [pointing to the Yaque]; even if you buy a plantain that was grown in the south, you can buy the plantain because we are taking care of this water."[4] As I discuss in Chapter 1, the possibilities for well-being in La Ciénaga have long been linked with forest policy, which has historically attempted to shape and reshape the local economy according to various national and international pressures. The rural economy was disrupted by the elimination of slash-and-burn agriculture, the operation and later closing of corporate sawmills, and the growth of large agribusiness. Tourism and conservation have evolved simultaneously and in an intertwined manner and, especially following the creation of the national park in 1956, have been sold as the panacea to the problems faced by community members. In this context, community subsistence and farming are the enemies of the forest. Cash-generating

4. These remarks are paraphrased from field notes.

activities, such as farming, and subsistence activities, such as the gathering of wood and medicinal plants in the reserve, "destroy" the forest.

While conservation measures have demonized subsistence practices and even led to legislation against them, the competitive and increasingly corporate and import-based Dominican agricultural market has made it impossible to live from small commercial farming. Tourism, by contrast, offers men an option. Tourism can transform male local residents into "protectors of the forest": they become guides (protectors), rather than farmers (enemies). Additionally, tourism requires no long-term time or cash investment and no land, and it gives immediate cash in return. This is extremely attractive to men, particularly young men, who do not have money to invest in seeds, fertilizer, pesticides, or transportation of products, and to the increasing numbers of men who do not own land at all. Finally, prior to incorporation into agricultural production, masculine peasant honor rested on men's ability as hunters and mountaineers, and a great deal of pride, especially for older guides, rests on knowing the ins and outs of the mountainside (see also Bonó 1968). Guide work offers men a reconnection to masculinity as it existed in the past, and as a hope for the future.

Women are also expected to protect the forest, yet the forest offers them a much less enticing friendship. Women are rarely the direct beneficiaries of tourism, so to recommend a transformation of the economy is to recommend the further marginalization of women. Conservation measures have restricted rural women's access to medicinal plants and fuel wood, and their control over household well-being is circumscribed by the increasing importance of a cash economy to which they have little or no access. What has been documented by feminist development scholarship around the world (Sen and Grown 1987) holds true in La Ciénaga: in an agricultural economy women were more able to handle household basic needs themselves. For instance, as Kata told me: "The life of a woman is being at home; she has to cook, she has to clean, she has to take care of the kids. That's her life because here there isn't even a [free-trade] zone for me to work in—you can't earn a living anywhere. You could only earn a living when there was coffee, you would go pick coffee—or when they planted beans, you would go and put in a day picking beans and earn a handful of beans. But now there is none of that. Now there is nothing for anyone." Their paid and unpaid labor in an agricultural economy gave women control over their basic needs, while a tourism economy, in Kata's assessment, provides "nothing for anyone." In other words, with people growing very little other than tayota, they are forced to depend on cash to buy food—and on men to earn it. In the early 1990s Foresta donated one hundred stoves and gas tanks to residents. This measure— meant to decrease dependence on the forest and, as a bonus, ease women's workload—took subsistence once again out of the hands of women. While they once could gather wood to ensure that food could be cooked for the family, now they rely on men's cash earnings to buy gas to fill the tanks. Conservation measures increase reliance on cash, and in an economy in which there are few opportunities for women, conservation measures increase women's reliance on men for subsistence.

TOURISM AND THE PROTECTION OF THE FOREST

Of the governmental and nongovernmental organizations (NGOs) with an ongoing presence in La Ciénaga, only one is not a conservation-based organization. In other words, the people are of concern only inasmuch as they affect the ecological space that they inhabit. NGOs concerned with conservation have been proponents of tourism and collaborated with the National Parks Department on training, trail maintenance, and even the placing of a two-year Peace Corps volunteer to work with the guides on national resource management. The presence of environmental and tourist organizations, combined with a history of demonization of local agricultural practices, has important implications for the way development is understood in La Ciénaga. In May 2000, I attended an "ecotourism" training for guides in La Ciénaga. The training was meant to be the first in a series to certify the guides as ecotourism guides. In this training they would receive information about first aid, sustainable development, and what might be called "customer service"—how to treat tourists. In the introduction, the director of national parks discussed the importance of tourism for the economy of the area and explicitly stated that tourism could eventually come to replace agricultural production as a means of subsistence for residents of La Ciénaga.

The hopes placed on tourism by both men and women are high. The interviews I conducted repeatedly suggested that tourism is seen as bene-ficial for the community. For instance, Jacinto stated, "When there is no tourism this place is dead. Because there is no production here—only the tayota and most of it through debts to the bank." Chela also discussed

tourism by contrasting it with the lack of possibilities of surviving through agriculture: "[The tourists] bring a lot of resources to the community. Whoever has a mule rents it and makes a little money, and when money comes into the community we all benefit. If this Armando Bermúdez Park did not exist, this Pico Duarte, the situations here would be much more sad. Because now the only thing we have is a lot of tayota planted and that is not yielding profit." Among those I interviewed there was only one exception to the speakers who communicated the sense that tourism was positive, a woman who claimed that all that tourists left was trash. Jesusita stated that tourism was "good for the people who go and earn some money, for those of us who don't, it isn't. All that's left for us is the trash they bring with them and toss around here." As I discuss later in this chapter, when benefits from tourism are available to women, they appear to be, upon first glance, mediated by men's relationships with tourists. Thus, for Jesusita, whose husband did not travel to Pico Duarte, it was unlikely that she would benefit either directly or indirectly from tourism.

While Jesusita was not involved in the tourist economy, there are ways in which women do participate. They sometimes host or cook for tourists or even rent a mule, if they have one. However, the work of housing and cooking is not formalized. While the guides have fixed park-sanctioned rates for guide work and mule rental, no such rate exists for cooking or

housing tourists. This is certainly consistent with the devaluing of household labor across the globe, as well as with the assumption that household
labor is an extension of women's natural being and, as such, does not
require cash compensation. The women of La Ciénaga often leave it at
the discretion of the tourists whether to pay or not to pay, although the
women do expect to be paid. In conversations with Cienagueras they
revealed not only that they expected to be paid (even when they told
people they did not), but also that they had clear ideas about what their
labor was worth. They often compared notes and were outraged by
tourist cheapness or impressed by generosity, but there was no formalized
way to ensure that their labor was compensated in a consistent manner.
To date, the National Parks Department, or Parques (Parks), as it is called,
has not proposed a way to integrate women into the local tourist economy. Conservation-Parks collaborations have worked with women on
small agriculture projects, but not on tourism—reinforcing the status of
men as wage earners while capping women's access to wages. However, it
should be noted that several kilometers downstream, women entered into
a restaurant project meant to formalize exactly these services. Sociologist
Claudia Scholz (2002) provides an excellent discussion of the challenges
encountered by this project.

EL ENLACE: THE GENDERED TOURIST-PATRON NETWORK

Thus far, I have tried to show that the historical relationship between
Cienaguera/os and discourses of conservation, coupled with the decreasing
possibilities for subsistence that is based on paid and unpaid agricultural
work, has increased local interest in the tourist economy in La Ciénaga.
This is the case despite the fact that the heavy tourist season is very short
(limited, for the most part, to January and Easter Week) and that the
income-earning possibilities for women are few and are generally mediated
by men's relationships to tourists. However, my data indicate that the tourist
economy is much more complicated than the exchange of money for
mules and a guide. Tourism has created a network among local guides and
middle- and upper-class Dominican ecotourists. I argue that the existence
of this gendered tourist-patron network, and the opportunities it implies, is
the third factor influencing local understandings of, and engagement with,
the tourist economy. The gendered tourist-patron network generates at

least two types of resources: first, immediate access to tourist money, and second, the formation of long-standing tourist-patron relationships.

The first resource, immediate access to tourist money, is understood as a combination of labor exchanged for cash, such as guide work or mule rental, and the "generous" gestures of tourists, such as handing a local child money or distributing sacks of food or used clothes. This "assistance" is often referred to in La Ciénaga as lo da'o and is understood as that which is not worked for, but given for free. The work women do, because of its lack of institutionalization within the tourist economy (and its devaluing in more general terms), straddles lo da'o and labor exchanged for cash. In other words, the work women do for tourists is not seen as work, and it is often not clear that it is being performed in exchange for cash. As a result, women are particularly vulnerable to accusations of being lazy or dependent on lo da'o. Moreover, because of women's limited access to paid work, they are more likely to use lo da'o as a primary source of well-being. I discuss this in detail below. While women's structural position within the local economy makes lo da'o particularly significant to their negotiation of well-being, when discussing the benefits of tourism for the region, men and women alike understood formal exchange and lo da'o as equally important, and the lines between the two were often blurred. The following observation was made by Chiquín in our interview:

> We didn't used to have the ties we do now. Now there have been a lot of changes, now a group of tourists comes, and what happens? The tourists like to make friends with kids and old people. They see a little kid hanging around and start playing around with him and almost any tourist takes out a hundred pesos—"Here, get yourself a piece of bread." That means that there is more development, we are improved, there is more development because there are more ways to earn a living, the atmosphere is better. There is more consciousness, we are more conscious about nature, about taking care of nature because that is what gives us life. That's why I see everything better.

In Chiquín's account, as in the tour-guide training, development is equated with consciousness about conservation and access to cash. Access to tourist money is understood as a "way to make a living." There is no distinction made between cash generated in formal exchange of mules or labor and that generated by the tourist's handing a child a hundred pesos. In other words the benefits of tourism are understood as a combination of formal labor and lo da'o, and when discussing progress in the community *the two are understood as equally important*. Moreover, the *enlace* Chiquín describes, and which I define as the gendered tourist-patron network, refers to "ties" with tourists both short term—as in the case above—and long term. I use the term *tourist-patron* to describe a group of people, generally Dominicans of middle- or upper-class background, who are frequent visitors to the park and who over the years have developed close relationships with their guides and guide families. Status and fame as a guide will influence the amount of *enlace* that you have, as well as your class position in the community.

When a neighbor invited me over for a can of Campbell's soup, because she figured that after two months I needed a change from the usual rice and beans, I learned that her husband, who was a guide, often brought home food items that were not consumed on trips. I later learned that the fringe benefits of trips included flashlights, boots, tents, backpacks—anything a tourist felt the guide might need. As guides developed relationships with tourists who returned once or twice a year, much more finely tuned systems of patronage were developed. This was especially true for older guides who had regular trips. One guide, Baltazar, spoke of his relationships with visitors from outside La Ciénaga: "I have worked a lot—I have lived many years with necessities galore. All of these kids, I have raised them struggling, struggling, struggling. The only thing I have, I am going to tell you, is that I am a millionaire without five cents because I have a lot of people. Lots of people all over, and where I have said, 'I need this,' nobody has ever said no. Thank God." For Baltazar, wealth is in his connections with networks of tourist-patrons on whom he is able to call in times of trouble. Another guide spoke of calling on a friend when a relative was in jail, and the friend/tourist was able to negotiate a lesser sentence for the relative. The *enlace,* therefore, is about more than cash: relationships with patron-tourists have also helped guides and guide families through yearly cash donations; assistance in finding kids jobs in the city; ways out of legal problems; support with medical bills; access to treatments, building materials, and so forth. These relationships involve access to resources and power, thus constituting an important local form of social capital (Bourdieu 1986; see also Auyero 2002). This is possible because of the many elite visitors, including military officers, politicians, and businesspeople, who frequent the park. As one resident put it during our interview: "A lot of important people have come here—truly, important people" (Aquí ha venido mucha gente grande—grande de verdad).

These resources and power available to Cienaguera/os are very much gendered. Several women I interviewed had spent part of their adolescence working, or working and studying, in the home of a tourist-patron in Santiago or the capital. Generally, they were "lent" (*prestada*) or "rented" (*alquilada*) as domestic workers when they were young girls between ten and fifteen years old and were "given" the opportunity to study ("Me dieron los estudios" [They gave me my education]).[5] Because schooling only reaches sixth grade, it is necessary to travel to continue education, and this is an expense few people in this area can cover. Assistance from a tourist-patron is one of the few ways to study beyond sixth grade. Sofía spoke of a tourist who has been traveling with her husband for years and has offered to take their daughter to Santo Domingo to study when she is old enough.

> Sofía: A man, one from [the capital] that travels with [my husband], those people said they were coming supposedly to look for her. Supposedly so she can start studying. Yeah, because he asked her, "What are your aspirations? What do you want to be?" And so she said, "Well, I aspire to be a cashier." And he says, "What makes you think"—because he, you see, didn't understand, and thought— thought that she meant she was aspiring to that now. She says, "I aspire to be a cashier"; he says, "And what makes you think a peasant girl"—because you see, in my house, look, [laughs] he is really a joker, my God! And anyone believes what he says—and he's joking around. He says, "What makes you think that a peasant girl can become a cashier, just like that, without studying?" And so [my husband] says: "No, she's saying that she is going to study for that." And he says, "Oh, well then, say that." He says, "Oh, I was not understanding."
>
> . . . He's supposedly going to come to get her when she finishes all her classes.
>
> LC: And will you let her go?

---

5. Martínez-Vergne's (2005) historical discussion provides some context for this practice of "adopting" a rural girl into the family to carry out household duties in exchange for an education and being treated as "part of the family." She suggests that this was also a marker of status within a certain class of urban Dominicans. This practice is common in other parts of Latin America and the Caribbean.

Sofia: [Silence] Well, I have to see, if—with—with whom one can send a girl outside of here.

LC: And is it to help her with her studies or to marry her?

Sofia: No, to help her study.

LC: He has his own family—

Sofia: [Interrupts] He treats us like—as if he were our son, that man. He travels with my husband to the Pico and one time he went to my house and he said to me, "You cannot have any more babies, you can't have any more kids." And he says, "Here, take this so that you can have yourself examined." He gave me five hundred pesos and he said, "I am going to pay for your sterilization." Look, you see him and you say . . . he's crazy is what he is. And each time he goes to my house he does not leave without leaving my husband a thousand pesos or two thousand. He has it, so he can do it.

LC: Are you going to have the operation with the five hundred or did you spend it?

Sofia: [Laughs] I spent it.

Clearly, as relationships develop, tourists become a part of the lives of Cienaguera/os and develop opinions about and claims on their lives. Sofia explains that the tourist's joking with the family, as well as his generosity, were signs of his close relationship with them. He took on the role of caretaker as if he were a son, and this relationship licensed him to have opinions about their lives, particularly the women's. Interestingly, his concern seemed to be with population control, a concern that is consistent with his own presumed love of nature as an ecotourist. Therefore, in this case, conservation of the land translates into control over women's bodies. For if the daughter studies, she can become a cashier (rather than a *muchacha de campo*) and avoid becoming a threat by having "too many" babies. The husband, however, as guide, is cast as protector of the land and thus the patronage he receives is not bound by the same terms and conditions. While the respondent is unsure whether she will send her daughter with the tourist-patron, and she used the sterilization money at her own discretion, she speaks of him and their relationship fondly. This can be seen through her repeated interruptions of her story to ensure that I will not misconstrue his intentions. In our conversation she accords him some degree of status as a son, both caretaker and patriarch, and as such

she defends his joking, but she regards the decisions about her body and her daughter as ultimately her own.

Chiquín, an older guide, also likened tourist-patron networks to family relationships. When I asked him how he and his family had benefited from the tourist industry, he responded: "I have a lot of tourists, but I have two or three that are from [the city]—one of them comes every year to bring me my Three Kings' gift. He brings me my envelope. He got attached to me one time that I took him to the Pico. That man thought that I was one of his kids. That check comes every Christmas with over a thousand pesos inside. I am extremely grateful to that man." Here again, the benefits of formal exchange and tourist-patron relationships are blurred because bonds of caring and affinity grow between a few regular tourists and residents. Chiquín, as a male guide, can benefit both from labor exchange and from tourist patronage. Whether residents truly come to regard tourists as family members, or feel that tourists regard them as family, cannot be known, but clearly some degree of mutual commitment, albeit within unequal relations of power, develops. I found this to be evident as I observed the interactions between several residents and long-standing tourists, as well as in observing how the absence of those who stopped visiting was felt and commented upon. It is important to note that tourist-patrons also stand to gain from their participation in gendered tourist-patron networks.

Tourist-patrons are guaranteed personalized attention when visiting the area, a sense of having participated in improving someone's quality of life, and, for many, the feeling of supporting unspoiled nature—the park—and what is seen by some as the "simple" and "humble" way of life that surrounds it.

GENDERED TOURIST–PATRON NETWORKS
AND COMMUNITY WELL–BEING

As I have discussed, there is no clear boundary between what is formal labor (cash for services) and what is "charity" when it comes to the benefits of tourism. And, as I have also argued, this is especially true for women's labor, which is not formalized in the way that male guide work is. Therefore, while there appear to be only marginal opportunities for women in the tourist economy, they have very high and particular stakes in tourist-patron networks. Additionally, while access to the tourist economy, such as mule rental or even cooking for tourists, is mediated by men's relationships to tourists, lo da'o represents an entry point for women that can be direct, and also directed by them independently from men. For these reasons, women have developed particular ways of engaging with tourist patronage, as well as with lo da'o more generally. I use the word *engagement* because I wish to complicate the notion of dependence on "charity/assistance." This dependence is not passive, nor is it passively accepted. Moreover, it is something that presents contradictions for residents of La Ciénaga, particularly those involved in community organizing, since at the local level it is seen to solve problems as well as create them. There is a dialectic between national projects, such as conservation projects, and local interpretations of conservation, development, and politics that creates a space for lo da'o and shapes Cienaguera/o common sense about work and progress. It is a myth to believe that getting things free is a passive process; as I will show below, getting things for free requires a great deal of work. Moreover, "free" things often come attached to strings that require accountability, action, or further negotiation (this can be seen above in Sofía's discussion). It is interesting to note that in universities, corporations, nonprofit agencies, and even freelance work, "getting things for free" is often called fund-raising, and entire offices exist to facilitate this process, which is coincidentally referred to as development. Yet for people who do not operate out of

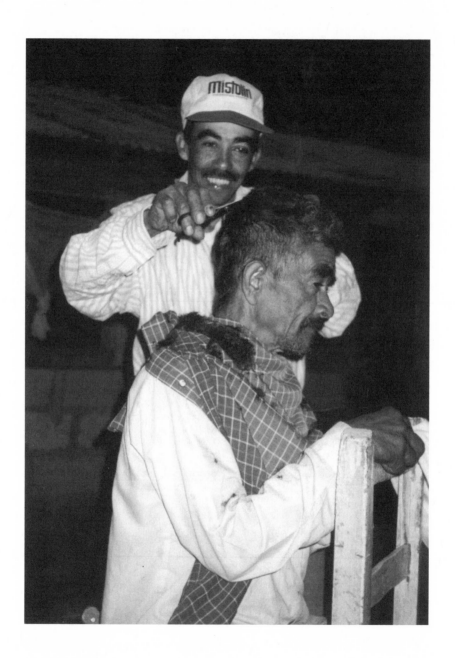

offices, it is called begging, dependence on charity, or a host of similarly unflattering names. In La Ciénaga getting things for free occurs on a personal and community scale. In fact, being a member of an association is, among other things, meant to ensure access to free stuff. Thus, being associated is especially useful for women, whose access to tourism is much more limited and thus requires creative entry points.

When Asociación Nueva Esperanza (ANE), the local women's association, wanted to build a new school, the Education Ministry required that the group buy the land itself. It was ANE that bought a plot of land and pressured the government to build a new school in La Ciénaga. Fundraising was done in a multipronged manner. Countless trips (on which a large sum of ANE funds was spent) to the municipal offices in a nearby town yielded some support, but not enough to finance the project. The local government, which promised to help finance the school, did not do so, because they felt the land was not adequate. So while the women were empowered to know their rights and the government agency responsible for their area, they were unable to get their funds through the formal channels for community development. The tourist economy proved to be an important source of funding for the school, which has now been completed.[6] Two of the women I interviewed spoke of raising funds by standing with a rope across the road that leads to the park and stopping tourist cars to explain their effort to build a school. Another woman whom I interviewed approached tourist-patrons, regulars with her husband, and got their financial support. The people she approached were carefully selected; in other words, she was not randomly asking people for contributions. Rafaela, the respondent quoted below, discussed how the money was raised and said she herself would not have been able to do what they did; she saw them as having special skills or character that enabled them to carry out fund-raising efforts for the school.

> We went back to work—let's ask this guy who can help us, "Hey, hey, can't you give us something more, let's see." Delegations were sent to the municipal office—the present representative— and supposedly he was going to give four thousand pesos, and we spent three thousand on the delegations, just to see. The Rotary Club gave us four thousand, they are starting to get involved here

---

6. The school, however, has not been built on the original land purchased by ANE.

[in this region]. Also another member—there were some doctors that traveled with her husband and she asked them, and right away they chipped in with six thousand pesos, that same day; boom-boom, right away they gave us the money. And that's how we were able to get the school here. Because if not, we were not going to build it. We were going to lose the opportunity. They told us, "If you don't have the land, we will go build it some-where else." And then what? Us left with nothing?

. . . So it was ask here, ask there—and we couldn't get the money together. The women, not me, because I am too shy, I cannot ask for stuff like that [laughing], I would die of embar-rassment. But Chela—they would hold a rope across the road and say, "Hey, hey, come on and cooperate with this!" Well, one person gave five hundred, another gave three hundred, and that is how we raised the twenty thousand to buy [the land].

These efforts are indicative of the amount of labor and the systematic approaches that are involved in raising funds. In the case of the school, tourism was tapped; that is, the women, whose access to the tourist economy is limited, found creative ways to obtain access to it. Ideally, in the eyes of many Cienaguera/os, being organized creates a different way of thinking about the tourist economy wherein the benefits of patronage can be filtered through an institution and more evenly distributed. And so when an organization or its leaders fail to do this, as I will discuss below, it is seen as a major shortcoming and is a frequent source of crit-icism of associations, including ANE, and their leadership.

HURRICANE GEORGE AND THE MOBILIZATION OF
TOURIST-PATRON ASSISTANCE

The benefits of tourism and the gendered tourist-patron networks are not limited to the tourist season. Largely as a result of local ties with tourists, politicians, and Cielo Abierto, a group of friends and tourists that became an NGO, residents of La Ciénaga were the recipients of a fair amount of assistance following Hurricane George in 1998, receiving zinc for roofs, food, water, medicine, clothing, and other items. Immediately following the hurricane, members of Cielo Abierto, who are very critical of lo da'o,

were at the forefront of hurricane relief efforts in La Ciénaga. Hurricane George became a structural opening for the negotiation of well-being; it represented a moment of increased access to resources that were always in demand and rarely made available in the community.[7] By making this argument I do not wish to underplay the very real crisis caused by Hurricane George. The losses were great. Large and small animals were killed; crops into which farmers had invested large loans were lost; homes, schools, roads, and bridges were completely destroyed. Thankfully, no human lives were lost—other regions of the country were not as fortunate. In the weeks following the hurricane no food or drinking water was available. Because the roads were destroyed, food could not be delivered to the colmados and the river water was not potable. The few crops that survived the storms could not be taken to market, because there was no road access; some tayota was taken down on mules, but the market price was not worth the expenses incurred on the trip. In the long run many farmers have not been able to repay the lenders for the crops they lost, and some have even found their mules being dragged away by angry debt collectors. National and international hurricane relief came by way of helicopter, mules, and human assembly lines (including several sets of tourists who

7. In addition, emergency relief came by way of international agencies such as the Red Cross and the U.S. Agency for International Development. I discuss these projects in the following chapter.

had mobilized to get supplies to residents) across the river, which is crossed numerous times to get to La Ciénaga.

The aftermath of the hurricane highlighted one of the significant problems that lo da'o represents for local organizations and outside NGOs. In interviews, many of the organized respondents (that is, members of associations) suggested that one of the major weaknesses of ANE was that the majority of its members only showed up when something was being given away. There was very low turnout for the bimonthly meetings or if there was work to be done. During the time period of my fieldwork, approximately twenty-five of the members attended meetings regularly and could be counted on for work. In other words, just more than a third of the membership could be considered "active." During the aftermath of the hurricane seven members left ANE, including four active members. The membership loss was the result of conflicts over zinc that was donated to the association for distribution among those who had lost all or part of their homes to the hurricane. The zinc dispute emerged in various interview narratives as a response to my inquiry about the successes and failures of ANE. Respondents from the coordinating body of ANE said that most of those who lost their homes were given zinc for their roofs, but that there was a gray area in which extra zinc was given to other members of the association. One respondent who left the association described the zinc dispute to me in detail, saying that while she was angry that she did not get zinc, she would have understood if it had really gone to the victims. Ester left the organization, not because she did not receive zinc, but because ANE leaders had given the zinc to people who did not need it, and who had not been associated or active as long as she had. She stated: "There were people who [a member] gave zinc to that sold the zinc because they didn't know what to do with it. So I was upset about that. One day they gave [another member] five sheets of zinc and right then she showed up right here in my own house trying to sell it to me because she knew I was doing this [building]." This respondent's own reading of the situation was that because she and her neighbors were *sureñas* (people from the south of the country), they were not valued as highly even though they had been members since ANE's inception.[8] These women felt that they

---

8. The word *sureñas* is also a racialized term that connotes "blackness," despite the fact that sureñas are lighter skinned than many Cienaguera/os. However, the sureñas I interviewed did not make reference to race and instead highlighted their position as "outsiders." For discussion of racialization in the Dominican Republic, see Torres-Saillant 1998.

were discriminated against in a time of crisis because of their status as "outsiders" in the community. Two current members of ANE brought up the zinc dispute in interviews, claiming that they did not get any zinc despite having significant losses. Both respondents said they did not leave the association, even though they were angry, because as one put it, "I am not associated to get free stuff." The implication is that those who left did so on the basis of not receiving zinc. However, those who left raised legitimate criticisms of the process, indicating that they did not leave merely because they did not get anything. Rather, it was the case that the distribution process reflected a hierarchy within the association, and within the community in general, that they found unacceptable. Even those who do not see free stuff as a primary reason to be associated do expect that the fair distribution of goods is the responsibility of the leadership. In this case, saying that members who left just wanted everything da'o became a way to dismiss possible shortcomings in the distribution process and inequalities within the community more generally. Similarly, presenting the notion that Cienaguera/os want everything da'o is an easy way for modernizing development discourses to dismiss the lack of resident participation in projects without engaging in critical examination of the value and appropriateness of the projects themselves.

So while disaster relief solved many problems following the hurricane, it created a fair number as well. It became a major point of crisis in ANE, and a faction of members was lost—active members who felt that they had been overlooked by the association in a time of crisis. According to many members of the community, one man alone (not a member of ANE) collected about two hundred sheets of zinc by tapping into his networks of tourist-patrons. According to some, it was by using the caricaturized discourses of nothing—by telling each person about his plight and claiming that he had not received any assistance at all. One elderly woman, Doña Luisa, told me, every time she saw me, throughout the entire year, that she was very sick and had not received any help ("Ninguna ayuda de nada"). In a conversation with an ANE leader, the elderly woman's name came up, and I said, "Oh yes, she is very sick, it seems, and she did not get any help for her house—she tells me that every time she sees me." The ANE leader laughed and responded that everyone joked about that woman and several other residents because they had a reputation for doing this. The leader felt that this made the rest of the community look bad. She said, "They'll even cry if they think someone who is not from here might help them." More than being an embarrassment, for this leader this presented a significant political problem, because she was responsible for fair distribution of the donations. To have people say they had not received help—when they had—undermined her credibility as a leader in her organization and community. In Chapter 3, I discuss the significance and uses of *nada*; I argue that while the discourses of nothing are, indeed, used to get free stuff, they are also points of critique that reflect the complicated relationship that residents have to visitors and projects.

CONCLUSION

In this chapter I have been concerned with how markets, conservation, ecotourism, and local lived practice have been articulated to create a local investment in tourism as the road to "progress" and "well-being" in La Ciénaga de Manabao. I have addressed two related questions: How can the investment in tourism in La Ciénaga, in the face of the seemingly limited returns it provides, be explained? And how do people whose means of livelihood (subsistence agriculture, small farming) is becoming increasingly displaced, and who choose not to migrate in search of work (in free-trade zones or service), meet their basic needs? To answer these questions I have taken on two powerful narratives in the development discourse of the region. The first is that residents of La Ciénaga are the enemies of the forest. Historically in the Dominican Republic, a good peasant, indeed a good (male) rural citizen, was a productive agricultural worker (Baud 1995; Rosario 1983; Gonzalez 1993; Turits 1997). Yet small-scale and subsistence farmers—who failed to produce large quantities for the market, were most likely employing swidden agricultural techniques, and had been driven increasingly closer to water sources in search of land and autonomy—were cast as a threat to the economy, the environment, and the nation. The criminalization of subsistence agriculture has woven itself with the discourses of conservation and ecotourism to create a narrative of rescue. In this narrative, local people are rescued from poverty and, simultaneously, the forest and the nation are rescued from them. However unable the rescue narrative is, in practice, to provide livelihood for a majority of the residents of La Ciénaga, it has helped create a space for ecotourism in "local knowledge" about work, development, and progress in the area.

The second important narrative I challenge is that Cienaguera/os do not want to work, and want everything da'o. This trope resonates with well-known, and still influential, modernist assumptions about the lack of "work ethic" of third-world, particularly third-world rural, peoples. My findings suggest that Cienaguera/os both work and want to work and that the more crucial question is, What constitutes worthwhile work? I argue that gendered tourist patronage—which emerges from and is enabled by the rescue narrative—is both hard work and worthwhile work. Tourist patronage, in the face of limited options, not only represents a significant stream of incoming resources, but also allows some area residents to negotiate the terms of their well-being. Sofia used the sterilization money she obtained from the tourist-patron on something else entirely. A school was deemed to be necessary by the residents, and so the money was raised. The zinc that arrived in La Ciénaga was distributed to those residents deemed to be most in need by the leader of the women's association. These examples indicate that women, in particular, employ patronage as a means to negotiate family and community well-being in a way that is simply not available to them through other channels. While this practice solves some problems, such as women's lack of access to resources, it creates and reinforces others, including existing inequalities based on class and status in the community. Moreover, tourist patronage allows the state to relinquish responsibility for the welfare of its citizenry, even while patronage is also a partial response to this problem. I do not argue that this is a practice that in the long run is sustainable, equitable, or just. What I do suggest is that analysis of gendered patronage helps answer questions about how local knowledges about development are created and work on the fringes of sanctioned capitalist exchange (see also Tsing 1993). The viability of various nontourist projects can be read as limited in part because of local investment in ecotourism—which has been created through the articulation of a variety of local, national, and global processes. This poses an interesting dilemma for development workers and certainly for development theorists. Additionally, it reveals how local people and local knowledge, the intended beneficiaries (or victims, depending on one's perspective) of development, do not simply participate or resist in the development landscape, but actively reshape and redefine its possibilities.

3

DISJUNCTURES:
WHY "NOTHING EVER COMES TO LA CIÉNAGA"

La Ciénaga is remote, but not quite forgotten. It is not quite forgotten because, as I have already stated, it is located in the buffer zone of a major national park that protects one of the most important sources of water for the country's agricultural lands—the Yaque watershed, or Cuenca Alta del Yaque. This location makes the area, and sometimes the residents, the targeted beneficiaries of a good deal of international funding, which is filtered through national nongovernmental organizations (NGOs). Almost all the NGOs and governmental organizations carrying out projects in the area are environment and conservation focused. They include a wide range of players, from the U.S. Agency for International Development (USAID) and the Nature Conservancy to powerful Dominican entities such as the Institúto Superior de Agricultura (ISA) and Foresta (the forestry service) to small NGOs such as Cielo Abierto. Between 1998 and 2001, I saw a variety of projects come to or through the area. These included a chicken coop project, a pottery project, a greenhouse, an ecotourism workshop for guides, rabbits, small vegetable gardens, latrines, aqueducts, coffee-improvement loans, bean-improvement loans, reforestation, a credit union, and an organic-farming course. Small-scale agricultural production and sustainability were at the center of the development agenda for this region.

In the early stages of my fieldwork, as I was trying to map the development landscape in the region, I often casually asked people what I thought was a fairly straightforward question: "What [development] projects are here in La Ciénaga?" To this question I most often received such answers as "My God, Light, *nothing ever* comes here!" (Adio, Light, aqui *nunca* llega nada) and "Jesús Christian! Almost nothing ever comes here" (¡Jesús Cristiana! Aqui casimente no llega nada). While this seemed an objective question that, I thought, should have a concrete answer such as "Well, the latrine, the greenhouse, the pottery," Cienaguera/os provided much more ambiguous answers, among them "Almost nothing." The more time I spent in the region, the more I became acquainted with the range of projects and organizations present in the area. A few Peace Corps volunteers, a couple of extension workers from environmental NGOs, and even several scientists from the United States turned up. Additionally, people began to talk about projects that were present or recently had been, though they were not as visible on a regular basis: a banking cooperative, a reforestation project, a bean-planting project, and a coffee-improvement project for crops, among several others. Given the quantity of stakeholders and projects in the region, why was I, like many other visitors, told repeatedly by residents that "nothing ever comes to La Ciénaga?"

To shed light on this interesting disjuncture between the myriad projects that appeared to be present but were reported to be absent, I will first analyze two distinct projects that I witnessed from beginning to end: the greenhouse and the sawmill. I will then discuss the process by which something might become nothing. Finally, using the example of the 2000 presidential elections, I will examine how "lack" is mobilized by Cienaguera/os as a strategy to secure well-being and also by politicians in an attempt to secure votes. I propose that the dominant narratives of absence or lack that characterize representations of local development, and that I term *the discourses of nothing,* are used in at least two important ways: as critique and as survival strategy.

TALE OF TWO PROJECTS

The greenhouse and sawmill projects represent different types of presence in the region and in the development landscape—a small NGO with a small international funding organization and a large international funding organization with a well-known Dominican NGO partner, respectively. Despite the differences between these projects, there are significant similarities in their impact on life in La Ciénaga. The greenhouse came through Cielo Abierto and a small informal Spanish NGO called Guaicaipura. This project was largely informal, loosely organized, and funded by a small organization rather than a large one. The sawmill (*sinfín*) project, which was funded by USAID after Hurricane George, came via Pro-Natura, an umbrella organization for a variety of environmentalist and conservationist groups in the Dominican Republic. I have chosen these two examples because they point to a pattern and show that the issues raised are not specific to a particular agency or type of agency.

We Asked for a Truck; They Gave Us a Greenhouse

One of the projects that I was able to see through from beginning to end was the greenhouse built in the summer of 2000. The greenhouse came through Cielo Abierto, which had been trying to receive funding from a Spanish NGO called Guaicaipura. Guaicaipura, an informal NGO with religious affiliations and access to funding in Spain, was composed of a small team of caring and energetic young people. The greenhouse was the first major project set up by Cielo Abierto. Before discussing Cienaguera/o discourses about, and engagement with, the greenhouse project, I would like to discuss the process by which the greenhouse arrived in La Ciénaga. Lisani, a member of Cielo Abierto, spoke to me about this process:

> We did not ask Guaicaipura for a greenhouse. The initial proposal that we presented Guaicaipura with was for a truck—transportation. It was because of the need that you see there (you know this), for transportation to come and go and move around outside the community and in the same way transport their [agricultural] products. So it was about seeing if we could, with this truck create a—a team, group, cooperative. They [ANE members] could manage a truck. I mean that was the first—that was the project we submitted to Guaicaipura.
>
> Guaicaipura was unable to find the money for that truck—so since we also had the need for a community worker and that was costing us a great deal, because it's expensive—just to live in the community—the trips, the bus tickets, it's a cost that we cannot

cover. So we submitted a proposal for a community worker, those were our priorities. But Guaicaipura says no, that they cannot fund community workers because the projects they fund have to be things you can see, things that stay with time [pause]; work with people stays, but you don't know how to measure it. You cannot take a picture of the work that happens inside people's heads—how their knowledge has grown or their way of thinking, I mean, you cannot take a picture of it and you cannot present it to those organizations. So they said they could not fund that either; that what they could do was this: a greenhouse.

Lourdes Bueno (1993) has pointed out that this problem of locally determined needs not matching with the funding priorities of donor institutions is a significant problem for rural development projects in the Dominican Republic. Gauging from interviews with respondents and conversations with ANE members and ex-members, the work that Cielo Abierto had done best, with the help of the community worker whom they hired with money from their own pockets, was, indeed, to organize and empower community members. Although they were unable to photograph or measure this work, the residents' narratives were a testament. For example, as Chela put it in our interview: "We are very grateful to Cielo Abierto. They are the people who have most opened up our knowledge. We were scared of talking. Don't you see how I am talking face to face with you? But in those days even I would have been afraid to talk face to face with you. You would've asked me something—[back then] there were people that hid if they knew [someone] was coming around. They closed their door so that you couldn't see them and locked it." As difficult as this was for me to believe—I had arrived four years after the formation of ANE and knew the women to be generally quite vocal, empowered, and assertive—this sentiment was repeated by many members of ANE. Cielo Abierto had been working in the area, and unlike other organizations it had focused on empowerment, literacy, and community building. Ironically, feeling pressure to have *something* concrete, its members chose a project that they were not prepared for, leaving them and myself wondering whether and when something is, in fact, better than nothing.

The project was set up, the dates for the arrival of Guaicaipura were announced, and the community was informed of the plans to build a greenhouse. Because I had spent most of my time in La Ciénaga during the previous months, I learned of the greenhouse and all the details at the ANE–Cielo Abierto meetings along with Cienaguera/os. In subsequent weeks I was invited to attend several planning meetings with Cielo Abierto in Santo Domingo. During the planning meetings, I mentioned that on the basis of the information given in the ANE–Cielo Abierto meetings, I felt that we—the residents of La Ciénaga who had been present at the ANE meetings and myself—did not clearly understand the greenhouse project. However, in the joint ANE–Cielo Abierto meetings, community members did not ask many questions and clearly voiced that they were in favor of building the greenhouse. When I asked ANE members about this outside the meetings, several said, "Que lo hagan" (Sure, *they* should build it [emphasis mine]), and told me that its purpose was to protect crops from the sun and rain. However, not one person spoke of why it would be beneficial. When the women's association leadership checked with the local agronomist, he said he saw no need for a greenhouse in the area. Upon the arrival of Guaicaipura to La Ciénaga, there was a brief meeting during which Cielo Abierto introduced the group to ANE and reminded people that this greenhouse (the greenhouse that came instead of a truck) was "of the community." Therefore, all association members should work with Guaicaipura, or "los españoles," as they came to be called, who had come such a long way to support the community.

In the second week of work, there were only a handful of community members participating in the building of the greenhouse. When I asked other residents, those who had not turned up to work, about the project, they unequivocally said they thought it was "very important." The general understanding of the uses of the greenhouse remained murky. So while there was funding and labor available from outside the community, the community was not "giving importance" to the project, even though, when asked, they spoke of its importance. In informal conversations with one male community leader (not a member of ANE) whom I visited on a regular basis, he told me he thought the greenhouse was very important and a good project. When I carried out a recorded interview with him I asked about the greenhouse.

> LC: What about the greenhouse work, what do you think of it?
> Jacinto: I see it as a good thing. Because as long as [pause] I don't

know [pause] . . . There is one in Jarabacoa. Well, I think that no, at least here, I don't think it has a future. Here in this spot, here in La Ciénaga. This is not the spot to have made that. [Gets very quiet and pensive. I wait out the silence] Because what is that for? To grow plants?

LC: A nursery . . .

Jacinto: Just like they came from Spain to make that greenhouse, they could have brought the resources to keep it up, to get the nursery started and help the growers plant. Because what I think is that they made the greenhouse but the resources are not here, because the association doesn't have them and they are not here. I don't see it being successful—why? Because those women, I'm going to call them the women, are going to begin to plant the plants but they are going to get tired. When they plant one thousand, two thousand plants and are fertilizing. [Pause] I don't see it, I don't see it, I don't see it.

The discussion with Jacinto reveals several things. Among them, unfortunately, is his lack of faith in ANE: despite the fact that there are several men in ANE, he calls the members of the organization "those women," insinuating that perhaps had the project gone to the (largely defunct) men's agricultural association, the project would be more viable. Moreover, he started by saying that he thought the greenhouse was a good project, as he had done in the past. While he knew what the greenhouse was used for, he did not understand the project—what were the goals and objectives of building the greenhouse? And beyond that, with what resources would the greenhouse be maintained? I had the same questions as Jacinto's, and the problem with this particular project was that *there were no plans* beyond building the greenhouse. The construction would be done by Guaicaipura during its one-month summer vacation. Thus, in some ways the greenhouse resembled the tourist patronage that is common practice in La Ciénaga. It was a one-time donation made by visitors to the park.

Money and supplies are only a part of what a development project means. People have hopes about the future of their communities; it is necessary to talk about them, to talk about how and why and whether the project of a greenhouse might be a part of those hopes. Despite the fact that Cielo Abierto members felt pressured into the project, they did genuinely believe that something good could come of it, that a use could be found for it. In fact, they held a brainstorming session with an agronomist who specialized in organic production and was familiar with the area. I was also present at this meeting and was encouraged by his optimism. Nevertheless, the initial problem remained: there had been no conversation with ANE about its members' (not to mention "the community's") own needs, desires, and visions for the future. There was simply the assumption that once the project began it was the responsibility of all to rally support. Several times I heard both Guaicaipura and Cielo Abierto remind ANE members, "Remember, this is yours, this is for you." The merits of a greenhouse aside, how and by what process is it of the community? It was neither born nor bred in La Ciénaga; it was handed over full grown and the community was asked to sacrifice itself to bathe, clothe, and love it as its own.

Hurricane Relief: "The President Came with a Sawmill"

Cielo Abierto members were extremely self-reflexive about the process by which the greenhouse had arrived and about their role in a project that went against their principles as an organization. And while they primarily faulted their lack of experience and outside pressures, it is important to note that the issues that emerged are not unique to them as members of a small, inexperienced, and poorly funded NGO. Following Hurricane George, long-standing conservation interests teamed up with emergency-funding agencies to create relief projects, including latrines and aqueducts. One of the projects that emerged from the crisis and had a significant impact on the area was the sawmill project run by Pro-Natura. The project, funded by USAID, was meant to help community members rebuild their homes by giving them access to the trees that were knocked down by the hurricane. The fallen trees had been immediately marked by Foresta with a red *F* and made off-limits to the residents. I was unable to find out what happened to this wood, though some was still on the side of the winding dirt roads more than a year after the hurricane. The Pro-Natura project to set up a sawmill in La Ciénaga—and, later, in several other communities in the Manabao area—was intended to facilitate local access to lumber at reduced costs. Additionally, Foresta, Junta Yaque, and each local sponsoring association (ANE in La Ciénaga) would be given a percentage of the money made by the sawmill. The idea was that residents would be granted permission (not otherwise available) to take the trees damaged by the hurricane and have them sawed into plywood at a low cost.

In reality, very few people were able to benefit from the sawmill. In interviews many people said that the sawmill was beneficial for the community. However, many of the same respondents, as well as other people I spoke to informally, said they were unable to saw wood, they lost money sawing wood, or they were forced to sell a great deal of the wood to break even. This is because while the project was set up to help residents rebuild their homes, the cost of the process made it prohibitive for many. People paid to saw the wood, they paid to transport the wood (by oxen) from the forest to the sawmill, and they paid to transport the wood (by truck) from the sawmill to their home or property.

Among those who sawed wood on credit were Rafaela and her husband. They had wood sawed for themselves, thinking they would sell part of it to break even, but they have not been able to sell any of it. They have not been able to pay for the sawing services and while they try to sell the wood, Rafaela must face the inquiries of the collector—an extension worker for one of the sponsoring organizations. Rafaela explains to me in an interview: "Look at our situation here—look at that wood sitting there, and Franco keeps coming to look for me [to charge me] and I tell him 'Look, get a truck and take the wood,' because there simply isn't any [money]. I don't ever leave here because of that wood—the hoodlums will take it." Since Rafaela's husband spends most of his time in the fields, she is forced to negotiate the visits from the collector, and moreover, as she states, her mobility is restricted by the responsibility of making sure nobody steals the wood. The project adds to her workload and intensifies the problem of debt that most residents already face—debt to the colmados for daily food, debt to the wholesalers for pesticides, seeds, and fertilizers, and now debt to Pro-Natura for sawmill services.

Despite the fact that this was a common problem that people shared informally with me, all but two respondents *in the context of our formal interviews* said the sawmill was beneficial. One explanation might be that while they felt it did not benefit them personally, they saw it as benefiting the community as a whole, or perhaps they felt that if they criticized the project it would either be ended or they would lose any possibility of such a project returning. I lean toward the second explanation, especially in light of the contentious relationship between Foresta and Cienagueros, Foresta's history of eliminating forest access to residents, and the repressive tactics with which they have enforced laws. I asked Jesusita how she felt about the sawmill project.

> Jesusita: I've seen it as a good thing, because it helps people, even if one is not able to [benefit]. . . . Look, there is a teeny tiny bit of wood, I don't know what I am going to do with it.
> LC: So you were able to benefit from it?
> Jesusita: Yes, jeez, because that is a benefit for the whole community. Look, I was just saying that had never happened here before, that a president came with a sawmill without one putting anything in to bring it. Right? I find that good—better than good.

While Jesusita herself suggests that she did not benefit—all she got a was a "teeny tiny" bit of wood—she sees the project as beneficial for the community because there had never been that kind of access. This access, when compared to the repressive measures of previous administrations, was interpreted as a generous gesture, which made a level of gratitude (and certainly not public criticism) the most appropriate response to the project. This would be especially important if continued possibilities for access were desired; clearly, in a context where permits must be received to access wood, these possibilities were desired.

It is important to note that there were several individuals who benefited quite a bit from the sawmill. The people who had access to resources, such as owners of oxen or trucks and those who had savings, were able to make a business out of this international-aid project. In La Ciénaga, a local man who owned a team of oxen purchased the wood that his neighbors were forced to sell in order to pay for ox rental, truck rental, and the sawmill costs, and he resold the lumber at market value in a nearby town! Thus, a structural opening for access to resources became a business opportunity and helped reinforce class differences within the community. This is indicative of the heterogeneity of interests among community members themselves. In this case, an NGO project meant to provide opportunities for a marginal rural community created a space for those with more resources to exploit many people who had lost their homes to Hurricane George. In La Ciénaga many people sawed wood on credit, hoping to sell all or part of it, but have not been able repay their debt. Because of these debts to Pro-Natura, ANE has not been able to collect its share of the profits. Clearly, there is not a monolithic community with unified interests. As is the case with tourism, structural openings for negotiating well-being were met with many competing interests and while some problems are solved, others are created.

Both the greenhouse and sawmill projects were represented as favorable, to me and to other visitors to La Ciénaga, yet they were overwhelmingly not perceived or experienced as favorable by Cienaguera/os. It is this disjuncture that interests me. The greenhouse was not desired or understood, and the sawmill, on the whole, created debt and reinforced structures of inequality. But in both cases, my questions were happening during or shortly after the projects, and residents, who often feel and describe themselves as "forgotten," wanted to maintain positive relationships to projects, thus keeping possibilities for future projects open. *Something is better than nothing.* This is particularly understandable given what sociologist Claudia Scholz describes as the "conspicuous absence of government services in the entire region" (2002, 32). An examination of how "nothing ever comes here" is deployed reveals the following critiques: (1) what is deemed necessary or has been explicitly asked for by community members has not come, (2) the projects that have come have not been adequately planned or supported in the long term, and (3) what has come has exacerbated existing inequalities and maybe even created new ones. All these criticisms might qualify a project to pass eventually from the "something is better than nothing" category into the category of "nothing at all."

HOW SOMETHING BECOMES NOTHING

Certainly these problems are not unique to La Ciénaga. Feminists and critical development theorists have been criticizing top-down development as ineffective and, moreover, as negatively affecting local communities. Their critiques, as I discuss in Chapter 1, have turned the developmental gaze toward local knowledge as institutions have attempted to center the voices of poor people, indigenous people, and women. Local knowledge, then, is seen as something that, once tapped, can create good development. Is it possible that centering local knowledge in the planning of these and other projects can make them better projects? And if this is the case, what is local knowledge and how do we obtain access to it as researchers or practitioners of development? It is to these questions that I now turn.

During the time when I was carrying out fieldwork in La Ciénaga, the United Nations World Food Program (PMA) was distributing food rations to residents in exchange for labor. On a walk through La Ciénaga, I went to the home of Digna and Fausto and had a cup of coffee. They had both been interviewed by a PMA researcher named Beth who was gathering data on local perceptions of the PMA project, information that could presumably be centered in future projects. Fausto and Digna were a couple in their late forties who lived primarily off their tayota crops and were both active with the ANE. Fausto said he had told Beth that he was very happy with the program—the food quality was good, quantity good, distribution good, and so forth. Digna, by contrast, had told the researcher that she got too little oil, that the rice never cooked right, and that she had no idea what to do with the wheat. Digna argued that Beth (with whom she had more contact than did Fausto) was on their side; she wanted to hear the truth, so that the program could be improved. Fausto, though he shared Digna's opinion about the food (too little, poor quality, of questionable use), insisted that if they complained, the program would be ended rather than improved. Something, at least, is better than nothing. Both had strategic reasons for answering the questions in a particular way. Both had an interpretation of Beth's agenda, and of the mechanisms of development in general, and this informed the answers they provided. Both understood that in the context of La Ciénaga, where it is extraordinarily difficult to put food on the table, a work-food exchange project was an invaluable resource. And both, alas, wanted my opinion.

I colloquially pled the Fifth: "Ustedes son los que saben" (You know better than I), I said. They both seemed to have a point. Mostly, I was too preoccupied with a new revelation to focus on the conversation; I realized that just as it was for Beth, what people told me, and what they did not tell me, also reflected the analytical work being done on me and my research by my "research subjects."[1] Their strategizing undermined my idea that because I was a researcher who listened, who cared what they thought, and even wanted to "center it," I would be presented with their knowledge and happily proceed to write many books and articles. As a

---

1. Analysis of my intentions shifted from person to person and throughout time. Things *I heard* ranged from "She's not doing anything" (No está en nada) to "She's writing a book" (Está escribiendo un libro). Both of these statements may have meant the same thing to many, and certainly both rang true for me at different points during my time in the field.

feminist critical ethnographer, a mixed-race U.S. Latina, I would "share my power," "open a space for the subjects to speak," "give them voice," and several other noble things researchers do. But Cienaguera/os have voice, they claim voice, and they use it selectively, just as I do—voice has never been mine or anyone's to give.[2]

The tension that emerges in Digna and Fausto's conversation—how to talk frankly and critically about development projects in the context of extreme poverty and radically unequal power relationships—is quite pertinent to an analysis of the *discourses of nothing*. In La Ciénaga open critique is perceived to be (and may well be) very risky, and though detailed examination lies outside of the scope of this book, the aftershock of Trujillo's repressive and brutal regime cannot be underestimated. While researchers and NGO workers do not represent the authority or inspire the fear that Trujillo did, it is clear that analyses of power and critiques of the status quo shape people's responses: power configurations are clearly read and actions decided accordingly.

There were other Cienaguera/os who, like Digna, were more explicitly critical of development projects. In an interview with Rafael, a community leader in his early seventies, I asked about the projects present in La Ciénaga. He said, "Nobody is bringing any projects here, what they are bringing is money to pay technicians." In other words, the Peace Corps volunteers, the extension workers, the agronomist who made visits to the community were the visible dimension of projects, and their presence caused me to regard them, as well as the projects they represented, as "something." However, they were not always following up on projects, or it was unclear just what their role was. The Peace Corps volunteer stationed in La Ciénaga was full of energy and desire to carry out the trail management project she was sent to do, but was neither receiving funding nor bureaucratic support from her supervisor to carry out the project. Moreover, she faced the challenge of establishing legitimacy as a guide and trail manager in a context in which this was considered men's work.

2. That we have the responsibility to engage with the voices even though we operate within a structure of unequal global power relations is another matter—as is the fact that we must struggle against this structure and against our own demons, which might allow us to believe that those voices are not feminist or strategic or analytical. My thinking on this is very much influenced by Diane Wolf (1996); Cynthia Wood (2001); several conversations with Lorena García; and, most important, "Digna," "Fausto," and the many other Cienaguera/os who have been interested in and willing to engage with me, and probably also those who have not!

In an interview with Jesus and Emilio, the two men had the following to say about development projects in La Ciénaga.

> LC: Have a lot of projects come here?
> Jesus: Oh yes, too many . . . and not— [Emilio interrupts]
> Emilio: They have not given results.
> Jesus: The projects here give very few results, they used to give us lots of work—they've gotten tired—well [ANE] is the one that has most—but they used to present us with a lot of projects.
>
> Well, lots of projects, supposedly to plant coffee, to plant oranges, and well, one time they brought coffee, oranges—those oranges right there—that was a project that came from the man who built that school [the Arraiján school]—but they never came back; supposedly they were going to give us [funding] for the maintenance of the oranges and everything. They never came back. Projects have come supposedly to lend us money, supposedly to improve the soil, to plant. It's like the project people say: "The money is ready, the money is coming," and that's the last you ever heard from them.

As Emilio and Jesus describe, many residents have experienced development projects as making unfulfilled plans and promises. "The money is ready," or as I heard while I was in La Ciénaga, "We are writing a project for a restaurant" (that never arrives), or "We have received a large sum of money from the Germans" (that never makes it to La Ciénaga). Many of these plans do not materialize or receive follow-up—"and that's the last you heard from them" (Y nunca se supo mas). Chela also spoke to me about the frustration of Cienaguera/os with outside development organizations: "They only offer—that they are going to administer, that they are going to bring this and that—but it never happens. People just come here to lie, because here they never follow through. They say—we are already sick and tired of promises and they never follow through. Not now. We [say,] why so many questions?—people are skeptical now, why so many questions they make you answer and nothing ever comes?" These experiences have undermined local morale and trust in projects. They have made Cienaguera/os lose interest in new projects and caused them to feel as though nothing much has come at all. In an interview,

Isabela told me that there were almost no projects in La Ciénaga. She responded to my further probing:

> LC: But I've been told about a coffee project for the women.
> Isabela: Yes, it came. But we didn't really place much importance on it.

So although some projects, such as the coffee project I inquired about, did in fact arrive, it was "not given importance." Here the answer "none" means "we (the women) did not give it importance" because it did not fit into the women's vision of development or their daily routine. Later interviews and conversations yielded clearer information about various projects, revealing disappointment with lack of follow-up and mistrust of sponsoring organizations. When I asked Isabela about another project that I knew was under way in the area, she confided, "I don't like the way [the project representative] operates," and about this same project, "They are using us." If there is mistrust about the project, it is unlikely that residents will give up control over their own schedule to participate, as is demanded by most projects. In other words, lack of participation, often read as laziness by the NGOs ("People in La Ciénaga don't want to work, they want everything given to them") is likely to be indicative of mistrust or conflicting visions of what worthwhile development is. This mistrust comes from analysis of the project (is it worthwhile?) and of the intentions of the project coordinators. These are just some of the grounds on which residents chose not to "give importance" to projects. Development organizations expect people to be grateful for projects—something is better than nothing—given the lack of options in La Ciénaga. But in this case, as in many others, something looked so much like nothing that it became impossible to rally the support of community members.

LUISA, BALAGUER, AND THE DISCOURSES OF
NOTHING AS SURVIVAL STRATEGY

In Chapter 2, I introduced Doña Luisa, who always reported to me that she was old, sick, and alone and that her house was falling down and she was not receiving any help from anyone. When I told one of the ANE leaders, she laughed at me and said that Doña Luisa told everyone that story to see what she might obtain. The truth is that she was, indeed, old, sick, alone, and living in a falling-down house, but these facts did not much distinguish her from many of her neighbors. The discourses of nothing were used, by Luisa and others, to obtain much-needed material goods and favors, particularly from political figures, as I will discuss later in this chapter. The ANE leadership, members of Cielo Abierto, and some community members expressed frustration with this practice, as it created conflict between association members. However, it is often an effective strategy because it pulls on visitors' sense of guilt and genuine desire to do something (*something is better than nothing*) and it fits nicely into what is an already developed system of tourist patronage and political clientelism. Additionally, Ricardo Vergara (1994) argues that to reap the benefits of international funding, you must show yourself to be in need of help, instead of portraying yourself as a capable citizen and agent. Clearly, proving victimhood by emphasizing lack, beyond an individual strategy, is an institutionalized practice required to obtain resources that structures of inequality put beyond your reach.

A woman who cooked for Guaicaipura managed, by the time the NGO left, to collect enough zinc to build a roof, the money to build a house, building materials, and land to build the house on. These were all out-of-pocket gifts from the young NGO workers, who grew close to her during their one-month stay and who, when interviewed, mentioned being moved by her plight (discourses of nothing). Cielo Abierto, who brought the NGO to La Ciénaga to build the greenhouse, felt frustrated because Cielo Abierto's work was being undermined. Maya, a member of Cielo Abierto, expressed frustration at this situation, which had caused a great deal of tension between the two organizations. When I asked her to identify the problem with the exchange, she sighed, then stated:

> The damage is losing credibility with the community on the one hand because you are talking about one thing and practicing another. Nothing more, nothing less. But that is a lot because you have spent four, five, six years talking about how they shouldn't beg, that takes away their dignity, that it just cannot be, that what they have to do is find a way to get things by their own efforts and then these people come, we bring them here and somebody gets the idea of telling them a sad story and they give [that person] a house. So then how are we going, I mean how

are they going to understand that? I mean that our blah, blah, blah is not worth a thing. That it is better to tell sad stories so that they can all get houses is evident.

Maya puts her finger on some key issues that this practice raises. While discourses of nothing sometimes make it possible for women and men to meet the most basic of needs, they create dependence rather than self-sufficiency, and members of Cielo Abierto, as long-term allies, have watched this practice create envy and conflict in La Ciénaga and thus have been extremely critical of lo da'o. My concern has been that getting free things requires work and certainly a great deal of thought, time, and initiative. While I share the criticism of assistentialism as a long-term development or transformative strategy, I worry that legitimate "dignified" work ("their own efforts"), as proposed by Cielo Abierto and other NGOs, is code for becoming good capitalists, indeed, "productive peasants." Individuals are being formally invited into a system that has been built on their exploitation and are being told that participating will make them more "dignified." Here the work of NGOs in subject constitution—in continuing the work of creating the good/serious peasant subject—is clear. And, perhaps providing the subject of another study, it is evidence that even innovative and progressive allies struggle against powerful and historical modernization and development narratives (Saldaña-Portillo 2003).

POLITICAL CAMPAIGNING AND THE DISCOURSES OF NOTHING

Thus far, I have been interested in how well-being is understood and negotiated by residents of La Ciénaga in a shifting global economy that increasingly displaces them as they interact with NGOs, state agencies, environmentalist concerns, and ecotourists. The presidential elections in 2000 proved to represent another key structural opening during which the discourses of nothing were mobilized. In La Ciénaga, politicians and local officials are often on the listening end of the discourses of nothing and, in fact, seek patronage relationships with which they attempt to ensure the vote of campesinos. Therefore, especially during election times, these discourses of nothing are used both by campesinos to negotiate well-being and by politicians to negotiate votes. In other words, campaigning officials say, "We know you don't have a sewing machine, wheelchair, house, pig, blender, box of diapers, or dentures, and we will buy it/them for you if you vote for our party."[3] Do campesinos sell their votes? The assumption of the politicians, and many Dominicans I spoke to, seemed to be that campesinos, rather than analytical and informed voters, are easily bought off.[4] Additionally, during elections, concern over the appeal of lo da'o circulated widely—because the assumption was that Cienaguera/os like to get things for free, rather than work for them, and logically the highest-bidding candidate would win the presidential election. However, I found that people were neither dupes nor easily bought off; moreover, the elections further revealed the labor demanded by attempts to secure lo da'o.

Elections in the Dominican Republic have a history of including bribes to voters, from small appliances to political appointments. Some parties are known for their "generosity" during campaign times, as was the case for Joaquín Balaguer. Balaguer, a candidate in the 2000 elections, was a trusted adviser to Trujillo; briefly president after Trujillo's assassination; and then president again from 1966 to 1974 and 1986 to 1994. Balaguer was especially well known for understanding the importance of peasant consent, which he achieved through means that included "land reform" and bribes, from food to construction materials, that were given out especially but not exclusively during election times. In fact, when I asked one resident her thoughts on lo da'o she said that Balaguer "accustomed us to that." Rafael put it another way, in reference to the Reformista Party: "The Reformistas were humanitarians." The 2000 election was no exception. When campaigning went into full swing, it represented a key structural opening for community members to negotiate well-being. Whether this meant trying to secure a job with the new government, cement to finish construction on a house, a wheelchair, or—one of the more creative examples—an amplifier for the local *bachata* group, several community members were working hard to get free stuff.[5] The amplifier case exemplifies the kind of intense labor that can go into getting free stuff, even during campaign time.

---

3. These are things promised or given out during the time I was there.

4. Scholarship on the subject of populism and patron-client politics across Latin America casts voters in a similar vein. For a critique, see Javier Auyero 1999, 2002. Like Auyero, I found the relationships between poor citizens, rural in this case, and politicians were much more complex than traditional understandings of clientelism assume. However, I found that the expectations for support associated with favors and material goods were perceived as much more explicit in the case of La Ciénaga.

5. *Bachata* is a traditional Dominican musical form that now has transnational appeal.

The *bachata* group had been planning to raise money to buy an amplifier. They often played at local parties and at most special occasions. The
musicians asked the local Reformista Party representative to help them get
the amplifier; they also requested help with the amplifier from Cielo
Abierto, which agreed to price amplifiers. Additionally, many visitors
were told about the amplifier in the hopes that they would contribute to
the cause of the musicians. The Reformistas promised that should they
win, they would provide the musicians with the equipment. Because of
this promise, the group's leader became actively involved in local politics
and attended various rallies as far away as the capital. Several of the
members traveled to La Vega to get quotes on the amplifier and to meet
with other party representatives, investing a considerable amount of time
and money in doing so. It is crucial to note that the days spent campaigning
or traveling were workdays and that the musicians were also guides and
farmers, and one was a mason.

Each day represented a workday lost, so it was indeed a tradeoff. Additionally, the group members took on the job of local campaigning, voicing
political opinions, and convincing other voters to support them so that
they could get the amplifier. All along they were told that the amplifier
was already bought—all they had to do was wait for the Reformista Party
to win to pick it up. In the end the Reformistas lost; as a result, the musicians did not get their amplifier. In a discussion with a neighbor in La
Ciénaga about the idea of people selling their votes, she said, "Sssaa, I
only trust one of them." She, of course, had no way of knowing how the
musicians voted, but her comment indicates that it was not unimaginable
for someone to vote for one side while campaigning for the opposition.
She added that if politicians offered her certain things she needed, she
would definitely agree to vote for them, but would never actually do it.
This idea of using political campaigning to the advantage of the voters
was also evident in the way a short-term medical program—a weekend
of free medical care for poor communities sponsored by the party—was
used by Cienaguera/os. I went along for the ride and found hundreds of
people from the vicinity lined up to receive medical attention—a rare
opportunity for most people in these rural communities. On the ride
back, we all joked over the fact that most of the passengers crowded
together in the back of the Reformista truck that had been sent to pick us
up—about thirty in this trip—were not Reformistas, but members of the
opposing Partido Revolucionario Dominicano (PRD). Nevertheless, they

chanted, "Y vuelve, y vuelve" (Balaguer returns!) for Balaguer while, with a wink, they held up their thumbs—the symbol of the PRD. In both these instances, campaigning can be understood as a strategy for meeting basic needs, not as selling votes under the assumption that campesinos are easily bought off.

When I asked Sofía how she felt about the fact that politicians gave items away as a strategy for getting votes, she replied: "Well, I see it as a good thing. Because there are a lot of people in need, a lot of people in need, and if they give them something, you see, now, they have to take advantage because after election time nobody is going to give them a thing. Nobody—look, none of the three [parties], no matter who wins." Emilio said that none of the main parties had worried about campesinos, and further: "This very government forgot about poor people. The man [Leonel Fernandez, the president] is a good man, we aren't going to tell you that he is bad. But he forgot about the poor." Emilio's description of Fernandez is interesting, because of its seeming diplomacy. His wording is that he is *not going to tell me* that Leonel Fernandez is a bad person even though he has forgotten about the poor. This wording was repeatedly used in interviews and conversations, especially when speaking about Trujillo. The statement "I am not going to tell you he was a bad man" often introduced a veiled, but discernable, criticism. Both these responses point to the lack of faith that Cienaguera/os have in party politics.

It was through an election-time conversation around an oil lamp–lit table where I sat with several men and women playing cards that I came closer to understanding how Cienaguera/os made sense of elections. Several of those present were trying to convince one man that he should vote for a particular candidate, and I asked why he should not just vote for the candidate he thought would do the best job. One man, twenty-eight-year-old Arturo, responded quickly—slightly irritated with me: "No, Light, we cannot vote like that here. Here we have to vote for somebody that we know, for the party of a local person, somebody that is going to be able to help us out if we need it here. Because it doesn't matter who is the president, that makes no difference here in this campo [rural area], they will never do a thing for us."[6] I stood corrected. Despite their lack of faith in party politics, *a lack of faith based on analysis,* they make clear choices—largely *based on local politics,* rather than national—about

6. This is a paraphrase of his comment, taken from my field notes.

whom to vote for and why. Discourses of nothing are used in politics in ways that are more complicated than is evident at first sight. That is to say, votes are not clearly sold, nor are the nothing discourses one-sided; both the voters and politicians use them as they navigate their way through election times. Although the example of the elections is different from that of the greenhouse and the sawmill project, I use it to show that discourses of nothing reflect points of analysis, rather than lack of interest in improving the quality of life of individuals and the community as a whole.

CONCLUSION

Despite the presence of development and conservation projects in the area, "lack" in La Ciénaga is quite literal and palpable. Therefore, it is probable that "nothing ever comes here" might sometimes just mean "I'm hungry." However, when that is all that is heard, as is often the case, too much is missed. That residents create narratives about development ("The greenhouse is very important") or tell sad stories ("Nothing ever comes here") is as important in understanding the nature of global inequalities as is statistical information on health, poverty, or literacy. It is also a testament to agency, to the complexity of local knowledge, and to the ways in which voice is claimed. "Local knowledge" is not innocent or authentic knowledge to be gleaned by the researcher who listens hard enough and carefully enough. The narratives reveal that local knowledge is not folklore or idiosyncrasy, but a means of seeing and acting in the world that responds to the material and historical conditions through which local actors have been formed. It is thus both analytical and strategically used. And when researchers, development workers, and politicians enter a development landscape that is characterized by unequal power relations, this knowledge is filtered by local people and should be. While I am not arguing that we, as researchers, NGO workers, allies, and tourists, should not continue to change and develop our tools for listening (and acting!), ultimately what needs to change are the very terms of the conversation.

4

COLLISIONS:
MEANING, MOBILITY, AND THE SERIOUS WOMAN

Thus far, I have tried to show the dynamic and mutually constitutive relationship between discourses of development and conservation, local definitions of progress and well-being, and Cienaguera/o agency. I have shown that throughout Dominican history there have been numerous efforts to curtail peasant mobility in order to transform peasant subsistence practices into "productive" agricultural practices. In other words, there has been a pronounced investment in peasant *immobility* as a defining characteristic of good peasant citizenship. As I have previously discussed, this has been a key source of tension as peasants have attempted to negotiate well-being in ways that are not always defined by capitalist productivity. In this chapter, I examine how women in La Ciénaga understand the continued investment in their immobility, how they struggle against it, and how in doing so they reframe the terms of their daily practices, while simultaneously challenging historically crafted tropes of good womanhood. I argue that centering these *collisions of meaning*—dynamic moments of confrontation between historical tropes and lived understandings—provides a way to reconceptualize gender in Latin America and the Caribbean in a manner that is both material and cultural and that unsettles accounts that continue to bind women to place, history, or tradition.[1]

1. Scholarship that has looked at gendering as a process provides an important opening for challenging gender as static. See, for instance, Salzinger 2003 and Suárez Findlay 1999.

MOBILITY AND GLOBALIZATION

As I discussed in Chapter 1, the changing global economy now depends not on the immobility, but rather the *mobility,* of the peasantry, particularly women. Women, whose options for income generation in rural areas are limited, migrate at higher rates than those of men and find employment in free-trade zones and the tourist and service industries in the Dominican Republic, as well as in Puerto Rico and the United States (Brennan 2004; Weyland 2005). In fact, in La Ciénaga itself, men outnumber women, as many women have left to find work in urban areas. Recent studies have focused on how these migrations, particularly in relation to the free-trade zones, transform women and families. These studies have shown the contradictory impact of free-trade zones—for instance, while working conditions in the zones are exploitative, they provide possibilities for women's increased empowerment and autonomy as wage earners (Finlay 1989; Piñeda 1990; Safa 1995b). A second set of important studies on gender in the Dominican Republic have focused on the contours of women as workers in key segments of the new global economy, including sex tourism (Brennan 2004), nontraditional agriculture (Raynolds 2001, 2002), and microenterprise (Blumberg 2001; Grasmuck and Espinal 1997, 2001). These findings have important implications for women as they work to secure well-being. For instance, as Blumberg (2001) and Grasmuck and Espinal (1997, 2001) argue, the success of women's microentrepreneurial activity cannot be measured solely in financial terms, because part of women's success lies not in income generation, but in the transformation of gender relationships within the family.

Many of these studies privilege wage work as an object of study and source of empowerment, and thus they also tend to understand the women who work and migrate as agents. However, a narrow focus on wage work erases women who do not enter the paid labor force or migrate, and it flattens the complexity of women's rich lives. Moreover, often studies that privilege wage work as a source of empowerment reify a nonagentic "traditional Dominican woman" with which these new entrepreneurial or mobile women can be contrasted.

In this chapter I focus on women who either stay in La Ciénaga or return there and attempt to create well-being for themselves and their community. I discuss some of the challenges faced by women who work, study, and organize, thus widening the lens through which Dominican women's mobility is understood and simultaneously placing women's wage labor into a larger context of struggles over gender meaning and well-being. The collisions of meaning that occur as women are confronted with the patriarchal investment in their immobility empirically reveal a great deal about the workings of gender and about how gender knowledge is created.[2] Additionally, shedding light on the moments when women's experiences collide with historically and geographically situated constructions not only unsettles notions of "traditional (local) gender roles" and passive women, but also provides a language with which to talk about the power of the gender constructs over expectations often placed on both women and men.

CONSTRUCTING THE SERIOUS WOMAN

Peasant women's labor in the Dominican Republic has always transcended the home (Brea and Duarte 1999; Guerrero 1991). Slave women worked

---

2. These collisions of meaning can be seen as part of what Gramsci refers to as "wars of position," or battles over meaning, that are carried out in the everyday realm of civil society (Forgacs 2000).

in the sugarcane fields, in other agriculture, and as vendors in markets (Albert 1993; Momsen 1993; Pau et al. 1987). Momsen (1993) has argued that because of this history of slavery, Caribbean women's mobility has been less restricted than that of women in other parts of Latin America. Additionally, she suggests that given this history, which often involved the severing of family units, women's dependence on men has also been less significant than elsewhere. However, as I discuss in Chapter 2, the female counterpart to the immobile "productive male peasant" construct has been the immobile, but not productive by definition, "good woman/serious woman." She has not been *defined* by her productivity, though she has always been productive, but rather by her immobility and, by extension, her reproductive work. As I discussed in the Introduction, expectations for "good womanhood" were based on possibilities for immobility that only existed for elite women (Martínez-Vergne 2005). During the Trujillo regime these expectations were written into laws. For instance: "Law No. 360 'which concedes complete capacity for civil rights to Dominican women,' also legislated husbands as heads of household and a gendered hierarchy within the family. Men were granted such privileges as the choice of residence for their family and even the right to prohibit their wives from working when they believed that it conflicted with 'the interests of the family'" (Turits 1997, citing Law No. 390, December 10, 1940, *Gaceta Oficial*). In his discussion of the Trujillo regime, Turits also describes the existence of regulations to encourage marriage and paternal responsibility and to regulate prostitution. These laws, ostensibly used to protect women's honor, also restricted their mobility, creating a sharp division between the "good woman" and the "street woman": "'Women had to be centered in the house, those that were house women. And those that were street women were in the street.' (Women during those days were thus perceived by [Turit's interviewee] then as either houseworkers or prostitutes)" (Turits 1997, 641, quoting a 1992 interview). Martínez-Vergne (2005) suggests that historically these divisions were also racialized and this certainly provided a foundation for Trujillo to build upon. As a vehement white supremacist, Trujillo was committed to whitening the nation through discourse, immigration, and genocide.[3] His racial project included eliminating all

3. Perhaps most widely known is the 1937 massacre that exposed Trujillo in a national incident. This massacre was the extreme expression of Trujillo's ongoing project to perpetuate racism and anti-Haitian sentiment among Dominicans. It is estimated that twenty-five thousand Haitians and black Dominicans were executed.

vestiges of Haitian and African influences in the nation; in the Cibao in particular, he worked to create the white peasant construct through immigration and outlawing Afro-peasant practices (Paulino 2005). Thus, while there was a history of women working outside the home—based on the experiences of slave women, and later free black and mixed-race women, indeed, most non-elite Dominican women—women's activity outside the home, particularly during Trujillo's regime, was simultaneously racialized and made sexually suspect. Like the "productive (white male) peasant," the "mujer seria" *was a discursive construct* created to stand in as the opposite of the laboring woman, who was presumably black.

The dichotomization between good/serious woman and prostitute/sexualized woman and the conflation of the working or mobile ("street") woman with a negatively sexualized woman continues today. The question of who is or is not a "mujer seria" was one that I repeatedly encountered in La Ciénaga. *Seria* and *serio* are terms used to describe women and men, respectively, who are thought to be upstanding and responsible. However, women I interviewed associated lack of seriousness in women with sexual behavior outside marriage and with theft; for example, Kata told me that a bad woman is a woman who desires a man other than her husband ("una mujer que tiene su esposo y quiere otro"). In an interview, Ester made a distinction between serious women and bad women, and I asked her to define the two.

> Ester: A serious woman is one that only desires/wants her husband. That's what we call serious. Or maybe that she doesn't touch what doesn't belong to her. That is serious.
> LC: And what is a bad woman?
> Ester: A bad woman here is the title people give [a woman] who lives taking different men. Having different relations not with the same [man]. Or maybe that you put down this glass here and shortly after she comes along and takes it and it's not hers. That's what we call bad.

However, she also states that women get called "mala," by both men and women, not because of their behavior, but as a result of resentment felt toward them because they are clean (not in work clothes) and well dressed ("quizá por que tu andes limpia"), or because men are attracted to them. This indicates that although there is some degree of agreement

about the definition of *mala,* there is also recognition that it is used to discipline women (in the case mentioned, for being too clean or attractive).
To be clean and well dressed (*andar limpia*) in La Ciénaga implies that you
have access to resources, probably through your own efforts; that you are
free from housework, farming, or other work that would keep you dirty;
and that you have somewhere to go (outside the boundaries of your home).
In short, to be clean implies mobility, independence, and neglect of reproductive duties; such behavior in women is suspect, and thus subject to
discipline. Thus, while Momsen (1993) has suggested that Afro-Caribbean
women are less bound by the investment in "women's roles" and "women's
place" because they have always participated in labor outside the home,
this does not ring true in La Ciénaga, where women are black, white,
and mixed race. Instead, even today, in a national economy that thrives
on, indeed relies on, women's mobility (especially to free-trade zones,
urban areas, and abroad), peasant women find themselves negotiating
their mobility and their subsistence.

LAS MECÁNICAS

One of the only opportunities for paid employment for women in La
Ciénaga is as day laborers at a nearby coffee plantation, or *finca.* Work at
the finca demands mobility, because it is located about five kilometers
away. The finca grows coffee for export. The employees of the plantation
are primarily Haitian and live in the finca. At coffee harvest, during the
time that I was in La Ciénaga, there was a group of about seven or eight
Cienagueras who worked at the finca as day laborers. There were another
two or three who worked as cooks, preparing lunch for the workers.
Cienaguero men are not interested in this work because of the low pay.
The women make 75 pesos (U.S.$4) a day and lunch. This is compared
with the men's 100- to 150-peso (U.S.$6–8) earnings as agricultural day
laborers or guides. Although this work is available only sporadically, the
men are unwilling to work for the 75 pesos that Cienagueras and Haitians
(both men and women) work for. When I asked the Cienagueras about
their relationship with the Haitian workers, they did not report negative
feelings toward them (though anti-Haitian remarks and jokes were well
integrated into local discourse). However, two women reported that the
only problem with Haitians is that they work for very little and thus drive

down the price of the women's labor. The women at the finca are of all ages; they range from single women in their late teens and early twenties to married women in their late thirties to grandmothers in their late fifties.

On the women's walk home, they passed several colmados where men tended to gather. These men, many of whom are single, landless, and young, have no land on which to grow their own crops, and while they work as guides or day laborers when there is work available, they spend a considerable amount of time hanging around between jobs. Looking for entertainment, they began to taunt the women as the latter came down from the finca and entered the village. The *coro* (chorus/running joke, as the women called it) went something like this: the men started yelling out as the women passed, "Here come the mechanics!" (¡Ahí vienen las mecánicas!). (Just what did this mean? I wondered.) It is important to contexualize this interaction by pointing out that in Latin America and the Caribbean, it is a normal occurrence for there to be commentary as women pass men on the street—"Adio, mami" (Hello/good-bye, mami), "Llevame contigo, belleza" (Take me with you, beautiful), and so on. Sometimes these *piropos* are flattering, sometimes sexually explicit or degrading, but mostly a bit of a nuisance. However, it seems that in this case, the men crossed the line of acceptable/tolerable commentary with the women who worked at the finca.

I remember running into one of the young women, Lisset, as I was on my way to visit a neighbor and hearing about "mecánicas" for the first time. Lisset was livid. She explained to me that she had gone to the local police and reported the harassment that the women were experiencing and that one of the young men had been arrested. I asked what was meant by "mechanics," and she said, "They say we are mechanics because we come down from work with our backs all dirty because 'no mas andamos debajo de los capataces'" (All we do is lie under our bosses)— like mechanics lie under cars. In other words, the men created a double meaning for *mechanic* to draw attention to the women's dirty clothing— the result of taxing agricultural labor—and to suggest that the women were involved in sexual relationships with their bosses. Lisset explained that she had had the young man arrested for saying that, and that he was being held, but his mother was begging Lisset to go and have him released. It seemed to me that this man was a friend of hers, and so I asked whether that was the case, and she said yes, "he's even a distant relative" (hasta familia viene siendo).

The arrest was merely the breaking point of a situation that had been escalating. Even prior to the *mecánicas* incident, the men had been harassing the women, calling them "cueros" (whores) and accusing them of sleeping with their supervisors at the finca. In other words, the men drew on the sexualized trope of the "street woman" to challenge the women's mobility. The men's taunts reveal that the women's sexual virtue and faithfulness to their husbands, in the case of married women, became suspect by the mere fact of their employment. And while all the women were implicated and outraged during the time of the incident, the man arrested was released (at Lisset's request) and the scandal over the arrest soon blew over. The men *did* quiet down.

As I found out from the interviews, the women had been fighting back even before the arrest. As Isabela, a married woman in her late thirties who worked at the finca, reported to me in our interview:

> Most young people don't work here. They don't work because their parents have gotten them used to slacking. Slacking and getting food without working. So the ones that are yelling stuff out like that don't even have five cents in their pockets. So we would go and work up there; they had the little joke of the *mecánicas*. . . . Sometimes I would get pissed—ah no! One day on my way home I was not in a good mood and that day I said, if today—the first one to say a thing to me today I will whack with this bottle, and I picked up a bottle of Brugal [Dominican rum]. When I come up the little road with that bottle of Brugal and say to myself the first one to say anything is going to get whacked with this bottle, I don't care who it is. That day I was truly—with the kind of work you put in at the finca, working extremely hard—then for some good-for-nothing to be yelling out at you.

And Jorsey also described a confrontation with the men prior to the arrest:

> The *tigueres* started this little joke about us—and wherever we went it was the same stuff.[4] And the worst part was that when

---

4. For an interesting discussion of the multiple meanings of the word *tiguere*, specifically in the intersections of masculinity and politics, see Christian Krohn-Hansen 1996. In this context, I would translate Jorsey's usage as "good-for-nothings."

you know that you are working and other people are talking about you—you could kill anybody.

Look, one time Juan [starts in] and I threw a rock at him so hard that he fell like an avocado. He never said anything again. And the man who started the [*mecánicas*] thing. I called him over to the river alone and he denied everything—because if he would have admitted it was him, I would have punched him right there and then.

While the women were clearly very upset over the name calling, they also had an analysis of the interaction that helped them regain their dignity and justify their work:

I say that they are a lazy bunch they don't work and they don't have five cents in their pockets—there were times that I came down with seven hundred pesos in my pocket that I earned . . . and these guys down here . . . towards the end I didn't pay attention to them. And I say that I will not stop working, I keep working. While I am able to work, I work. Because the day I don't have anything to feed my kids I can go to the store and buy food on credit; they sell it to me because they know I am working, but if I am not working, they won't sell it to me on credit.

Interestingly, while the men draw on the sexualized "street woman" to degrade the women, Isabela reclaims her own good standing by drawing on discourses of the "indolent peasant." Her productivity and access to cash give her dignity and power vis-à-vis the men, "who don't have five cents in their pocket." Neither the women nor the men are particularly invested in living up to the gendered good-peasant construct (and the economy does not facilitate it), yet in this collision of meaning each uses it against the other as a way to reclaim power.

The *mecánicas* incident was not an isolated one, but one of several manifestations of men's insecurities about their role in women's lives—as both provider and "true love" on the individual level and as leaders and primary wage earners in the less individual sense. The men drew on the trope of "street woman" in an attempt to regain control of women's labor and mobility through the sexualization of their actions and choices. The women who worked at the finca (or worked in town, or organized, or studied, as I discuss below) posed an implicit threat to the status quo—they were asserting their mobility and their independence from men and in some ways from the confines of the community as a whole. In other words, while women have always worked in agriculture, these women were going beyond working at the farm of their uncle or brother or husband (many of whom are landless or can no longer compete on the food market); they were working for an outsider and for outside income. Additionally, some of these women who worked in the finca were single, and their independence appeared to put them out of the reach of the unemployed men. These men would not be able to provide the women with a house or furniture or land (considered an important criterion in a man, especially given the lack of opportunities for paid work for women), as a supervisor at the farm, for instance, might. This, in fact, is very likely one of the most crucial threats in the minds of Cienaguero men: that women's mobility has the potential to render them obsolete. Thus, the sexualized taunting was both a slap on the wrist for the women and a way for the men to regain power—if nothing else they had the power to get a reaction from the women, to make them mad and force them to engage with them. The women engaged in the power struggle, so on the one hand, they gave in by reacting, but on the other, as can be seen, they continued to work and did not sit back. They challenged the men and eventually (with the arrest of one young man) got them to back off.

Although the incident was manifested in culturally and historically specific ways, it is not geographically isolated. Ong (1987) and Mummert (1996), for instance, have documented that in Malaysia and Mexico, respectively, the increased mobility of women that results from entry into paid industrial and agricultural labor has opened them up to questions about their sexual behavior; this is expressed through gossip or taunting. One of the main vehicles regulating the way women live, love, and labor is gossip. Gossip floats somewhere between voices and silences, what is said and what is not said. It is an amorphous, yet oddly sharp, form of regulating the daily practices and sense-making of all Cienaguera/os, but particularly women. The above are parallel situations in which communities grasp for control, particularly over women's bodies, in the face of changing economies and dynamic sensibilities and meaning-making about how women should live their lives.

FORMAL EDUCATION AND WOMEN'S MOBILITY IN LA CIÉNAGA

It is difficult to get a formal education in La Ciénaga, and it is more difficult if you are a woman. This is because an education, especially beyond
sixth grade, involves a degree of mobility and financial resources that are
not readily available to young women. It is to the relationship between
women's mobility and education that I now turn. There are two schools,
one that goes up to sixth grade and a second one, recently built (see
Chapter 3), that is meant to provide classes through eighth grade. The
new school is the result of a great deal of organizing on the part of the
ANE, whose members were worried about the deteriorated conditions,
distance, and danger involved in getting kids to school (crossing the river
on makeshift tree-trunk bridges), especially during the rainy season.
Although most Cienaguera/o children today attend school through sixth
grade, this was not always the case. The majority of Cienaguera/o adults
are not literate; even when classes were given, many were not required
by their parents to attend (there was other work to be done), and others,
particularly women, were not permitted by their parents to attend.
Clara, a sixty-one-year-old Cienaguera, told me that she had wanted to
go to school but was not allowed to because her parents said that the
teacher was in love with her. Another sixty-one-year-old woman, Josela,
told me the following when I asked her about her formal schooling as a
young girl.

> Josela: I was in school for about four or five years and I didn't
> even learn the letter *A*. Not even the letter *A*. Because during
> that time my teacher, he was an older man, and he took to liking
> me so much and thinking so highly of me that he did not give
> me class. What I knew how to do was wash [clothes] and so what
> would he do? He gave me work so that I would wash his clothes.
> LC: During class time? That is an abuse!
> Josela: In school and he would send me to the river to wash his
> clothes—the river was right next to the school. And I would go
> and come back for a little bit of school and then go home.
> LC: And did he pay you?
> Josela: No, look, he gave me books, colored pencils, and note-
> books, he gave them to me, but he wasn't teaching me anything.

She states that the teacher thought highly of her and, since she claimed not to be a quick learner, he spared her having to spend time in school. While her parents sent her to school, and she wanted to learn, the teacher undermined her education by giving her the task of washing his clothes. Josela describes this as a very painful and frustrating experience and describes her struggle with literacy later as a young woman: "Each time I saw somebody reading, somebody reading a book, my eyes just wanted to fall out. I wanted to read. You know I made an offer to the Virgen del Carmen that she help me read so that I could do a holy hour for her, that I would read a holy hour to the Virgen del Carmen. Girl, three months later I knew how to read all kinds of things." Josela's struggle to teach herself how to read, confronting the limitations that were being placed on her by patriarchal notions of what she was "good for" and "good at," is echoed by women in younger generations. Likewise, Clara's story of her mobility and thus education being circumscribed by the investment in protecting her sexuality ("The teacher was in love with me") is echoed today. The constraints are especially evident when it comes to attending school beyond sixth grade. To go beyond sixth grade, several of the women study through a church-run radio program called Radio Santa María. The classes and assignments are broadcast and they go to class once a week. Additionally, several young men (from better economically positioned families) go to high school in Manabao, which is about twelve kilometers away. Both options involve expenses that few Cienaguera/os can cover, including transportation, food, supplies, and enrollment.

Miriam, a seventeen-year-old Cienaguera who was a top student through sixth grade, was not permitted to continue her education. While she wanted to study and was very bored at home, she had not been able to convince her mother to allow her to study. Since many young women her age are married and having kids, this increased her own isolation. Although other residents, particularly members of ANE (Miriam is one of the youngest active members), tried to encourage her mother to let her study, she replied that she doesn't trust the women who go to school because "you don't know what they are up to" (no se sabe en que andan). Once again, women's mobility leads to speculation about their activities and their virtue. However, clearly it is not only men who perpetuate this; mothers, sisters, and neighbors also serve to regulate one another, and to fight for one another as well. Chela, a thirty-three-year-old woman, and Jorsey, a twenty-one-year-old woman, each speak about how they have had to negotiate their education with their family and have found support with their respective partners:

> One day, she [her mother] was toasting coffee and I was sitting here behind her—she had her back to me and was looking at the pot.
>
> I say, "Mamá, I am going to enroll to study through Radio Santa María."
>
> She says, "To study, *mi'ja* [daughter]? I cannot have you studying through Radio Santa María."
>
> I say, "Mamá, what are you thinking? You have to let me study."
>
> She says, "Study?"
>
> I say, "Well, look, if you don't want me to study, grab that rope, you see that palm tree right there? Grab that rope and hang me so that I don't study. You don't even want to give me an education or anything."
>
> She says, "You are not going to study."
>
> And the only thing she did was swat me, *whap,* on the head [laughs]. That was what she did. And that's why today, now that I am married, now after I am married I repeated fifth grade and now I am in eighth. Because my husband has made it possible for me to study and I am always working wherever I can. I find money and when I don't have any he gives me some so that I can pay for transportation and eat. But back then, when I wanted to study—I wouldn't be studying now, I would have a profession. But how was I going to get that? They [my parents] said they were too poor and could not help me study or anything. The only thing I did was that when I was eighteen I had to get married to a man, and right away I started having kids.

Like Chela, Jorsey finds that it is her boyfriend who has supported her both emotionally and sometimes financially in her decision to study. She describes her confrontation with her father about her studies:

> Jorsey: If it were up to the parents, you wouldn't study. Because they don't even want you to go from here to there alone. But I said to Dad, "Dad, if you, if you don't want me to study, I will leave here."

LC: He didn't want you to study?

Jorsey: Dad did not. He said that if I went, in fact, when I was studying in Manabao through Radio Santa María, he would say, "If you keep going on Sundays, you will have to leave here [for good]." And I said, "Well, I am going to keep going, even if I have to leave." And later I met Francis. Francis encouraged me to keep studying, that he would help me with whatever and I enrolled.

LC: And you didn't feel that your dad would kick you out of the house?

Jorsey: No, I knew he wouldn't.

These examples, which span the experiences of three generations of women, indicate that there is clearly an investment in "women's place" and women's immobility. However, these collisions of meaning also indicate that this investment and the boundaries it implies are also continually being pushed and redefined by women through their lived practices. A second thing that becomes clear is that there is *no fixed role* for daughters, mothers, or husbands to play, as these relationships are also negotiated in the process. Jorsey's father attempted to restrict her mobility by threatening to kick her out of the house, but she stepped up to the challenge and kept studying, certain, as she stated, that he would not follow through. By not supporting her studies, he maintained the image of patriarchal control, even while her actions (she kept studying and did not leave) redefined their relationship. Likewise, male partners can at times be oppressive and at other times be key allies—and sometimes both things simultaneously. Development theorists and practitioners have these contradictions, among many others, to contend with when centering local knowledge, and women's knowledge specifically, in discussions of development.

MOBILITY AND THE NEGOTIATION OF FAMILY LIFE

Most women were faced with the challenge of meeting basic needs, sometimes as the head of the household, other times as the primary earner, and others as coprovider or supplementary provider. Most women I interviewed expressed interest in income earning and the creation of paid work for women in La Ciénaga. However, women also wanted to and did work, participate in projects, organize, and study, not just for money but also to improve the quality of their lives. As several women put it, they did these things "para embullarse en algo" (to have fun, to entertain yourself with something). Ester told me, in our interview, about a previous job, which I assumed was paid.

> Ester: I worked with this man they call [——]. I picked coffee and picked beans at the farm and filled up the bags.
> LC: Did they pay well?
> Ester: What pay? They gave us a pack of beans. We did it so we wouldn't be sitting around, at home with nothing to do. One went to pick, work as a day laborer, and when you were leaving they would say, "Take beans," and you, from a place three kilometers away and on foot, how much were you going to bring home? A tiny bit.
> LC: So you worked for the tiny bit of beans that they gave you or because—
> Ester: [Interrupts] To entertain yourself, to get out of the house.

Although the women had a great deal of work to do in and around the home, many found that outside work or projects (paid or unpaid), when done on their terms, broke the monotony of the daily routine. Research on women's participation in the cash economy indicates that women who generate their own cash not only are better able to meet basic needs, but also gain increased autonomy, mobility, and decision-making power within the home (Finlay 1989; Ong 1987; Safa 1985; Mummert 1996). While my findings echo this, they also raise questions about whether it is "income earning" per se that is responsible for women's increased well-being. Whether a result of income earning or the pleasure and empowerment of increased mobility and a change in routine (or a combination), these gains are not simple or easy, but require confronting and negotiating hostility and constraints from husbands, mothers, children, and neighbors. In other words, not only do the women have to juggle the labor they perform inside and outside the home, but they also must manage and finesse the emotions and expectations of male partners, children, and community members.

In oral history interviews I asked the women if their lives had changed after marriage, and there was a wealth of responses. Mobility is a theme that repeatedly emerged unsolicited. Some women felt they had much less work, some felt they had more, some learned to navigate the world, and some said that if they knew then what they know now, they never would have gotten married at all. Twenty-nine-year-old Ester spoke very lovingly of her husband, who is also her business partner in a small store that she started after participating in the literacy project with Cielo Abierto.

> Well, my life has changed a lot since marriage, I find that it has changed a lot. When I lived in my house, I did not even have a sip of beer, I did not go out. My dad did not let me go to a party, or dance. He did not even let me—well, sometimes if it was with an uncle or aunt and they were close to us he would let me go to a wake. But I did not have the same freedom I have now. I have more freedom now. . . . My D—Mom had more restrictions on me than the husband I have. I'm still thankful to him for that. Because a lot of times there are young women who are at home and have freedom with their parents and then they get married and their husbands don't give them freedom. But the opposite is true for me, my husband has given me freedom and my parents did not.

While Ester found more independence after marriage, her language suggests that this freedom is "given" by her husband. That it is "given" implies that there is some struggle, that it is not natural or the norm for her to have or demand this sort of mobility, but, rather, that it is something to be given or taken by forces outside her control. Ingrid, who is thirty-nine years old, speaks of the changes she has made in her life since marriage and motherhood.

> Yes, it changed. Because after one gets involved with a man, and has kids, she has to change her tune. If one likes to roam around, she has to prohibit herself from that a bit; one can roam, but not as much as when one is single. I also used to like to dance. I prohibited myself from that, all of that dancing stuff. I don't dance at all. No. Not because I don't like it, because I have a young lady and her father does not let her dance. So if she sees me dancing— when I go out I go out with her—if she sees me dancing she can say, "My mother is older than me and she dances." So I don't dance anymore, I don't give my daughter a bad example.

While Ingrid's mobility is now limited—she does not "roam" as she did when she was single, and she attributes this to marriage and motherhood—she states that *she herself "prohibits" herself* from going out, as well as from dancing, to set an example for her daughter. Again, Ingrid's language implies struggle—it is not that she does not want to dance, but that she feels she should prohibit herself from the activity. So like Ester, she implies that mobility is not automatically deserved or possible, but is, rather, the result of struggle (with oneself and others) because of the meanings attached to women's mobility. She goes on to state that she dances once in a while with her husband or a neighbor, but that she does not make a habit of dancing. Women's sense of responsibility for their children and their solidarity with them can also be used as a bargaining chip by men who wish to control women's mobility, as Angela, one of ANE's leaders, divulged:

> For me to go to a meeting we [my husband and I] have to talk way too much [beforehand]. "Where is it you are going? And those kids?" And this and that. . . . Right away he puts the kids in front of me. *Not himself,* no, the kids [she laughs]. And that's why I feel bad. Because one also has to step up to one's responsibilities and the men from the *campo* [rural area] are not like men who have studied. That if he, if the man has to stay at home and cook or do something he'll do it. . . . Ayy, Light, [she laughs] sometimes I get frustrated and say, *Ayy!!* But I can't just dump my family for the association.

In Ingrid's case she takes full responsibility for restricting her mobility out of a desire to be a role model for her children. We do not know exactly what role her husband has in this decision other than the fact that he does not allow his teenage daughter to dance. In the second example, Angela makes it clear that her husband attempts to limit her mobility by manipulating her commitment to her kids to intensify her own concerns about neglecting them because of her activism. While Angela often finds herself having to finesse her way to association meetings, trainings, and outings, she has remained extremely active. On the community level, she is a powerful and respected leader whom men and women seek out for advice and support; however, as is true for other women organizers in La Ciénaga, this adds tension to her home life. Both these examples draw on assumptions about the "good woman" being one who is close to home, a woman who does not flaunt her sexuality (for example, by dancing) and who carries out her reproductive duties to both her husband and her children. Historical tropes are clearly a force to be reckoned with.

By focusing on women who challenge expectations about their mobility, I do not want to suggest that women with limited mobility are passive or quiescent. As the following example illustrates, women engage in complex forms of resistance. I recall sitting in the kitchen with Adela and Flor. Flor was preparing dinner, peeling green bananas, and Adela and I sat on stools near the clay stove, Adela sitting with her youngest daughter glued to her lap, her tired braided head leaning heavily against Adela's chest. It was near night, the sky a dark gray, but the bright flames from the fire on which the bananas would cook lit the kitchen and the faces of my neighbors as we talked. We spoke of the ways in which women make money in La Ciénaga; it was not a conversation that I had started, but it was one that I had had many times. There were few options for women to earn an income in La Ciénaga, and several had recently left to work in the free-trade zones or in people's homes. The coffee plantation where several women worked was rumored to be on the brink of bankruptcy, and in any case, it was difficult for women with small children to work there. The women discussed the income-generating activities practiced by women, such as holding raffles, selling products (akin to selling Avon goods), and making sweets. Other entrepreneurial women made hot dogs or other snack foods to sell in the afternoons, particularly to the men who gathered at the colmados or to tourists. These were small markets, though, and certainly could not provide subsistence for the many women who needed it. When there was no money available, either because the men were not getting work or because they were not passing the earnings on to the household, the women found themselves having to obtain credit with the colmados (see also Flora and Santos 1985). Flor complained that it was very hard to be able to put food on the table and of being in debt to the colmados, of having to buy food on credit, and of not being able to count on her husband's income to cover basic needs. Adela sympathized, and she confessed, with a glimmer of pride and a fit of the giggles, that she often had to steal money from her husband to pay for the following day's food. He would simply refuse to give her the money, and she would wait until he went to the river to bathe and then would rummage in his pants pocket or, while he slept, sneak out of bed and over to his jeans as they hung from the beam that crossed the ceiling! The three of us laughed about this. Flor said that her husband took his pants with him to the shower. Unlike Adela's family, who bathed at the river, Flor's household shared a running-water pipe, surrounded by zinc and wood scraps, with approximately five other households, who also shared an outhouse. And when he slept? Flor comically described how her husband folded up his pants, with the money in his pockets, and carefully placed the pants under his pillow. There was no way she could have pulled off Adela's brand of spousal theft! Adela continued her story:

> Yeah, well, Hidalgo [her husband] started to realize that I was stealing money from him. I remember one time he asked me, "Adela, what happened to the hundred pesos I had in my pocket; you are a very good thief [*una ladrona fina*], aren't you?" I told him, "Well, you were out drinking and you know you keep all your money rolled up in your pocket; you probably dropped it somewhere." Pretty soon he got himself a little duffel bag with a little padlock and he would keep his money in there. But I figured out how to get in there too.[5]

[Flor and I laughed hysterically as she told her story. I must admit, my field note transcriptions do not do justice to the humor with which she told the story.]

> I would bunch up the zipper area and gently start pulling the two sides of the zipper open until I could reach in with my hand. [She smiles as she acts this out.] One time I pulled out five hundred pesos and I ran to the store first thing in the morning to buy a big can of [powdered] milk. When he realized the money was gone he came into the kitchen and asked where the money was. I pointed to the can of milk. He then yelled, "When are you going to stop stealing from me?" and I said, "When you start providing for your children!" He just walked out quietly. You know, I saved up enough money to buy a new stove that way.

5. This is paraphrased from my field notes written later that evening.

I cannot say how representative Adela's behavior is, as this conversation was with two women with whom I had developed close relationships, and they were thus particularly candid with me. However, Flor's husband's act of taking his pants with him to the shower and then sleeping with them under his pillow indicates that the threat existed, at the very least in his mind. I must also point out that the fact that Hidalgo "walked out quietly" was not representative. Adela and Hidalgo engaged in many violent fights and at several times throughout my time knowing the couple, one or the other had the bruises to show it. While I cannot say how representative stealing from husbands is as a strategy for meeting basic needs, I do think it speaks volumes of the way that women are not passively defined by systems of gender oppression. They challenge these systems in individual and sometimes collective ways.

ASOCIACIÓN NUEVA ESPERANZA AND THE
CHALLENGES OF WOMEN'S ORGANIZING IN LA CIÉNAGA

Women who stretched and redrew the boundaries of their mobility in La Ciénaga were open to many challenges. I do not mean to imply that women were bound to the community; many women left altogether, taking jobs in the capital or in Santiago, marrying outsiders, or even leaving the country. Some of these women, and most of the women (and men) I can think of, maintained close ties to their relatives and neighbors, providing stories and living examples for young women about the sorts of options that were available. What was tricky was choosing to stay in (or return to) La Ciénaga to push from the inside. When Cielo Abierto first began organizing in La Ciénaga, its members did not intend to organize primarily women. However, it was women who tended to show up at their events.

One of the first projects they carried out in La Ciénaga was a literacy campaign. When Javier, a member of Cielo Abierto, recounts how they began organizing women, he states: "The men were afraid to admit that they did not know, for instance, how to read or write. The women were more humble in that sense and they were willing to learn. And that's what they manifested. So, in fact, in the beginning the men would tease them, make fun of them. I mean, when they were inside, it was like a little school; they said—[the men] were on the outside saying things, making jokes." Adela, who along with several other women learned how to read and write with Cielo Abierto, also spoke about the men's reaction to the literacy program. She described the men standing outside looking in through the wood planks that held up the zinc roof, teasing the women and one another, saying that the women were learning how to read and write in order to write love letters to other men. The women were initially not taken seriously and were seen as just a group of gossips (*bochincheras*). Because of this they were kicked out of the community meeting place, a church, which was controlled by one of the male leaders in La Ciénaga. In response, they built their own meeting place down the road. In an interview with eighty-year-old Omer, one of the few men in ANE, he told me that the men used to say that the women were just a bunch of loudmouths (*escandalosas*). He continued: "Now they find them good, since those women, God, no association had reached the standing this one has reached. . . . The women are doing things well." The women have attained a high standing in the area. They have developed relationships with many outside organizations; they have built their own meeting place; they are the point of entry for almost every project that arrives in the area; and they are key contact persons for people who visit the region—politicians, journalists, and visitors. Nevertheless, despite the power they wield and respect they have earned, they have to continue to prove themselves both collectively and in their families in the face of attempts to undermine their respectability.

Despite the fact that ANE has come to take a prominent position in the community, or perhaps because of this, the members find that their struggle in the home intensifies. Several of the active women said their husbands were the primary obstacle they had to overcome in order to continue to carry out their work. As Angela put it, her husband was "the little problem [she] most feel[s]" (el problemita que yo mas siento). Adela and others echoed this, reporting that their husbands said that once women got involved in ANE the women were ruined (*dañadas*). The women said they were seen as ruined because they were busy, but also because they stood up to their husbands and did not put up with as much.

Jesusita, an ANE member in her sixties, brings these issues back to the realm of women's bodies and the links between women's mobility and women's perceived sexual promiscuity. When I asked what the shortcomings of the women's association have been, she offered the following:

> [The] women who have those husbands, that don't want women to go anywhere. . . . People, nobody eats people, you let yourself

be eaten if you want that. And if she [speaking of women in general] would not have wanted him, she wouldn't be with him, right? That is what I see in various, in all of them—they don't want to help the woman go out—help them [the men]—because the work they do is to help him. Whatever comes to the associations is also for him. . . . Men are jealous. They think that one— if one did not love them, one would not be with them. One is not thinking about bad things, one is thinking about raising the family.

Thus, for Jesusita, the biggest shortcoming of the association was not lack of membership, or resources, or cohesiveness, or even commitment, but rather the conflation of women's labor and mobility with sexual promiscuity. This distortion of women's attempts to improve their quality of life and that of their family and their community was what worried Jesusita most. If women write, it is to write love letters to another; if women go out of town, it is to meet another man; and if women work, they are sleeping with their bosses.

CONCLUSION

I have shown the gendered dimensions of the historical investment in peasant immobility. While the good peasant was the productive peasant, the good or serious woman was bound to the home. The workingwoman's mobility made her sexually suspect, in the same way that male-peasant mobility (hunting, foraging, and shifting agriculture) was stigmatized as indolent. Additionally, like the trope of the "indolent peasant," that of the street woman was associated with blackness—reflecting the racist underpinnings of development processes in the Dominican Republic, as well as elsewhere in Latin America. Despite these constructs, Dominican women have always worked outside the home, and today's global economy continues to demand and rely on women's mobility. Women who migrate internationally and provide remittances or work in tourism or the free-trade zones provide a significant part of the Dominican economy. In other words, women's mobility is restricted, but women still move. In this chapter I have focused on how women who chose to stay in or return to La Ciénaga, avoiding direct incorporation into free-trade zones or migrant economies, confront the continued investment in their immobility. What is illustrated by this analysis is that gender is not a static category and that it must be understood as continually redefined in the same way that local knowledge is redefined at the intersections of structure and agency.

Women are not agentic superheroes of resistance whose untainted (read: liberatory) knowledge will create good development (for critique, see Wood 2001 and Gordon 1997). They are not passive or silent, but they are living in and against a structure that seeks to define them and thus are negotiating pressures that are often contradictory. As individuals and as a collective, Cienagueras are actively searching for ways to eat and to feed their families, to find joy and pleasure and love and well-being. Very often this struggle is complicated because it is carried out with and against those people who most love and support them—parents, children, husbands, and neighbors. Through their daily practices, these women are waging the one thousand tiny "wars of position" that make up the fabric of culture and thereby creating new knowledge about the possibilities for women.

EPILOGUE

Inspired by what might be understood as the turn to the local in development studies, I began this project with the certainty that development and the capitalist world-system more generally must be understood, challenged, and transformed from the ground up and that the first step was to center "local knowledge." Local knowledge, for all its currency as a development buzzword, would not be found, and in its place instead was the messy reality of a wealth of competing logics and practices, dynamically constituted and in dialogue with structural forces. These logics are a cacophony that seems daunting, and perhaps their inconsistencies have always been obvious, but the lack of attention to their meaning in development theory and practice has created many blind spots and sometimes, I suspect, has precluded the elaboration of creative ways to support local self-determined struggles for well-being. Indeed, these logics reveal a great deal about the process by which economic development and nation-building create gendered peasant categories, but importantly, they also unsettle what we think we know about categories such as *peasant, woman, work,* and *progress.*

The encounters, disjunctures, and collisions analyzed in this book illustrate the historical underpinnings of the development discourses that are mobilized in conversations about development and environmental conservation in contemporary La Ciénaga. Cienagueras and Cienagueros are affected by global, national, and local development forces and they cooperate with, resist, and redefine the possibilities for development on a small and large scale, on the basis of their own practices and definitions of well-being. Local knowledge and agency often work in ways that scholars, activists, and development experts do not expect.

Analysis of the making of local knowledge helps illustrate that the global and local cannot be conceptualized as distinct categories—they can only be understood relationally. All of development's actors must be understood as both knowledge producers and persons who live in a marked tension with large economic processes and local lived practices and definitions of well-being. Thus serious engagement with culture, and the knowledge it reveals, is key to transforming development from a project of *rescue* to one in which alliances are forged in a multilevel struggle against global inequalities. Deromanticizing development's presumed beneficiaries and representing them in fuller (yet never in their full) complexity renders the rescue approach ineffective and opens the door to new ways of envisioning the possibilities of a transformative development that is not about producing developed subjects, but about challenging inequalities and democratizing well-being.

I have focused specifically on local knowledge in La Ciénaga; the specifics of my findings, therefore, are not generalizable to other countries, towns, or even neighboring areas. For instance, on the other side of the Armando Bermúdez Park, where tourists have not been an active force, one can assume that the development landscape looks very different. Likewise, in Zambrana-Chacuey, unique environmental sensibilities have been shaped by an organized struggle over land (Rocheleau 2005). As a case study on the construction of local knowledge, this book reveals the subtle links between the historical development of the Dominican peasantry and the historically crafted identities that confront development and conservation politics today, and thus it presents a method that is certainly applicable to a variety of localities.

It is important that rural life and rural people do not disappear from the radar of scholars interested in how the shifting global economy is experienced, engaged, and shaped. In the Dominican Republic, as in other parts of Latin America, the Caribbean, and Central America, research and activist attention has privileged migrants, urban economies, free-trade zones, and, increasingly, large-scale international tourism, including sex tourism. While it is indisputable that these areas need to be understood, given global economic, political, and social trends, what of those women and men who do not migrate to urban areas or obtain employment in free-trade zones?

Jared Diamond (2005) has recently brought attention to the (controversial, though cast in a mostly favorable light by Diamond) environmental measures taken by both Trujillo and Balaguer, and Diamond has even explicitly mentioned the Vedado del Yaque (today's José Armando Bermúdez National Park). From a strictly conservationist standpoint, the high percentage of protected lands (30–32 percent) in the Dominican

Republic is noteworthy (Diamond 2005; Lynch 2006). However, the marginal rural communities affected by these measures receive only passing mention in Diamond's account. As "sustainability" (Baver and Lynch [2006, 4] point to its ambiguous definition) continues to secure its place on development agendas, as alternative and small-scale tourism and eco-tourism gain increasing popularity, as states continue to capitalize on nature and tourism as a source of income (Burac 2006; Miller 2006), and as food security is increasingly threatened for the many (Lynch 2006) while abundance is secured by the few, the ways in which rural liveli-hoods intersect with, are affected by, and shape economic development and environmental conservation need to be placed squarely on the agenda. Critical, poststructural, and feminist approaches to development and globalization have exposed the ways in which nations and peoples are enmeshed in a complex web of power relations and difference, but retreat is an inadequate and equally fraught response. This is because, beyond commodity chains and global communications, what weaves us together—ties of blood, compassion, fear, distrust, imagination, hope, history, memory, pain, violence, desire, responsibility, potential to create something better—cannot easily be disentangled.

One of the things I have been interested in showing is that La Ciénaga is part of a development landscape made up of a variety of actors and forces—conservationists, Dominican and international tourists, politicians, elite agricultural interests, markets, NGOs—that affect daily living in this community. The interconnections that are exposed by using the Women, Culture, and Development approach, a "radical interactionist" approach to development studies, reveal the complexity of the landscape and of the players (Bhavnani, Foran, and Kurian 2003). These interconnections make it clear that alternative approaches to development must also be based on interconnections in the form of progressive alliances. Moreover, they suggest that the tourist, the traveler, and the seeming "outsider" have a role, indeed a responsibility, to enter into such alliances. Such alliances must have as their objective the transformation of systems of inequality, rather than the alleviation of poverty. And thus they must be based on partnership rather than paternalism—in other words, based on a politics of respect and not of rescue.

The data I have collected in La Ciénaga indicates that many residents want to work in partnership with outside organizations and in fact share many of the same objectives in the areas of health, education, work, empowerment, and agriculture. It is the process by which the variety of forces and actors would like to—are willing to—arrive at those objectives that must be worked through. This process requires transformations, and not only at the grassroots community level; alliances must operate on a variety of levels. Empowered subjects are crucial, but they are truly effective only in tandem with challenges made to the system locally, nationally, and globally.

The last formal theme covered in the interviews I conducted involved people's hopes, dreams, and desires for the future of La Ciénaga, and thus it seems most fitting for these to be shared by way of conclusion to this book.

Javier (Cielo Abierto member), midthirties

I wish I could know what the people in La Ciénaga, what their dream is—I've come to learn that mine doesn't matter so much—that was a lesson—it's theirs [that matters]. But mine would be that it become an economically self-sustainable community. Politically, not that it become its own little country, but that politically it can demand its rights from the authorities, from the state, from other organizations, and that it can come to understand what its future is and decide its future. Because as it is there are other people deciding for them. We [members of Cielo Abierto] are among them. And we have always thought it was a little dangerous and presumptuous because one is entering into their lives, one is transforming their lives. Of course my life is also being transformed by other people; it's being worked over by the political economy of this country, the global political economy. I don't know—not everyone sees it that way. So then we are trying to make, to produce this transformation of the community and of the individuals in the sense that they can become—produce their own income and live dignified lives and so too the future generations in La Ciénaga; one cannot hope to do more than that. The right to health, the right to education, the right to have fun, even the right to die in a dignified way.

Josefina, twenty-seven

Well, that we be able to find work here, that they send something, that they send food, because we live broke—we live struggling to eat. That people remember to bring something for us. I don't just want stuff for myself, just like one needs it, so do the others.

Chela, thirty-six

My wish for La Ciénaga is—to have our own vehicle for the association [ANE], and that we each have, the mothers of families, have a garden in our houses, so that when I make rice there are some vegetables there so we don't eat that rice plain because that is not nutritious. That is garbage that we are putting in our stomach. But if we put vegetables or something else in, we are putting some vitamins and minerals in. And in the future I want each person to have at least their little farm in their house with five chickens that lay eggs. That they don't have to go out and buy that, we need a lot of things here. Because here we have to buy everything, and how can one progress? Starches purchased. There are no beans? There is no corn? There is no nothing? There is no coffee? Only a little tayota.

Gracia, fifty-seven

Something that leaves a benefit, I would like cows.

Nestor, midthirties

I would like to see it replete, instead of weeds, that there be something, anything, planted. That the government make it possible for us, for me and for all the rest, so that we can plant and they guarantee us the markets.

Ester, twenty-nine

Well, my wish is that the kids be able to learn. That we could have the means to educate them. That we could have work, here in La Ciénaga there is no work. Very little because here the work there is, is almost all for men. The work for women is washing clothes—that is inside the home and one does not earn money that way.

Josela, sixty-one

My wish, I would say above all is for the road and for the bridge. And recovery, that La Ciénaga continue to recover. Those would be my wishes. Because you know that where visitors go the community improves, grows. People get here because we are right next to God, but not because these are roads fit to travel on.

Chiquín, seventy-two

I would like you to put the issues of the road and the bridge into your study—and that your study be a success.

Rita, twenty-eight

My wish is that the whole community be rich, that I be the only poor one, everyone rich and just little me poor, because if the community is rich and has—I can go mop the floors for this one and they'll give me a pound of rice, go to the other one and get two plantains. But if we are all poor where am I going to go? My wish is that everyone live well and that nobody be pulling in their own direction. That if you have the plantain and I have the beans—"Light, look, [have some] beans," "Look [have some] plantains"—and we share what there is between the two of us. I don't just want everything for myself, I want everyone to have the same thing.

Jacinto, almost seventy

The only thing I would need is to find a girl that would take me to the United States so I could finish out my old age over there.

Estela, late fifties

These folks are cooling off, because they think the world has forgotten them. My wish is that La Ciénaga move forward. That La Ciénaga move forward and that it grow in wealth and knowledge. That people know a lot and that in the future we see something, because if one lives this way, always squashed, squashed and you never see anything, you never have anything. [Estela then responds to my question "How would this be done? That it grow like that?"] *Adio!* People fighting. If people don't fight then nothing grows.

APPENDIX

THE STUDY

The ethnographic data on which this book is based was collected during fourteen months of fieldwork between 1998 and 2001 in Santo Domingo and La Ciénaga de Manabao. La Ciénaga is a small rural community; in all, there are about 350 households in La Ciénaga, and in Boca de los Ríos (the entrance to the park), where I spent the majority of my time, there are forty households. I lived full-time in the Dominican Republic from September 1999 through August 2000 (with the exception of the month of June). Until February 2000 I was primarily based in Santo Domingo and made frequent (three- or four-day) visits to La Ciénaga. Beginning in February I spent the majority of my time in La Ciénaga. Throughout my time in the field I participated actively in community life, particularly in the activities of ANE. This included everything from visiting neighbors and helping clean and sort beans to building the greenhouse and attending trainings, both in and outside La Ciénaga. It was this participant observation that provided a context from which I could make sense of the interviews I conducted with residents of La Ciénaga. I conducted forty-three tape-recorded interviews in total and two nonrecorded interviews (as a result of technical difficulties). Throughout the book I distinguish paraphrased material from verbatim transcripts (see Duneier 1999).

To protect the identity of respondents I have changed their names and, where necessary, identifying features, but I did not change the name of the community. While changing the names of villages and communities is a convention used by many ethnographers, my hope is that this research will provide not just a sociological study, but also historical documentation of a region about which little has been written. Additionally, it is my hope that the findings can be of use to Cienaguera/os, and to organizations that work in the area, as we all reflect on our goals and strategies for supporting self-determined well-being in La Ciénaga. I am only one of many outsiders involved in community life in La Ciénaga in one way or another, and it seemed important to remain accountable for the claims I make in this book. I have not changed the names of organizations working in the area, but I have changed the names of the representatives with whom I conducted informational interviews. When dealing with sensitive information given by these respondents, I preserve their anonymity by omitting the name of the organization.

The majority (twenty-six) of the forty-three taped interviews conducted were oral histories with residents of La Ciénaga, including both members of ANE and nonmembers. I carried out sixteen oral histories with members of ANE. To cover the breadth of perspectives and experiences, I created a quota sample to include members from different *parajes* (regions); various families, ages, and levels of participation; and both women and men. By the time I began interviewing people, I had already been visiting La Ciénaga for several months and was gaining a sense of the dynamics of ANE; a random sample could not have captured the diversity of perspectives that I knew made up the organization.

The remaining ten oral histories were with key informants. These were community members who were described or described themselves as particularly knowledgeable about the community and former members of ANE. Six of these informants were men and four were women. Eight of the informants were more than fifty years of age.

To contextualize development and conservation in La Ciénaga, and to document the variety of stakeholders and pressures that were present, I mapped the key organizations and interests in the area. These included nongovernmental organizations (NGOs), governmental and military offices and personnel, urban elites, long- and short-term tourists, environmental organizations, journalists, and scholars. I carried out thirteen informational interviews with a variety of persons representing these interests, though not all of them were taped. Finally, I spent a great deal of time with the members of Cielo Abierto (the urban counterpart to ANE), attended many of their meetings and trainings, and conducted in-depth, open-ended interviews with the four core members.

REFERENCES

Acosta-Belén, Edna, and Christine E. Bose. 1995. "Colonialism, Structural Subordination, and Empowerment: Women in the Development Process in Latin America and the Caribbean." In *Women in the Latin American Development Process,* edited by Edna Acosta-Belén and Christine E. Bose, 15–36. Philadelphia: Temple University Press.

Agaarwal, Bina. 1991. "Engendering the Environment Debate: Lessons from the Indian Subcontinent." CASID Distinguished Speaker Series, no. 8. East Lansing, Mich.: Center for Advanced Study of International Development.

Albert, Celsa Batista. 1989. *Los africanos y nuestra isla.* Santo Domingo, Dominican Republic: Ediciones Centro Dominicano de Estudias de la Educación.

———. 1993. *Mujer y esclavitud en Santo Domingo.* Santo Domingo, Dominican Republic: Ediciones Centro Dominicano de Estudias de la Educación.

Alonso, Ana María. 1992. "Gender, Power, and Historical Memory: Discourses of *Serrano* Resistance." In *Feminists Theorize the Political,* edited by Judith Butler and Joan W. Scott, 404–25. New York: Routledge.

Anderson, Benedict. 1991. *Imagined Communities.* New York: Verso.

Andújar, Carlos. 1999. *Identidad cultural y religiosidad popular.* Santo Domingo, Dominican Republic: Editora Cole.

Appelbaum, Richard P., and Gary Gereffi. 1994. "Power and Profits in the Apparel Commodity Chain." In *Global Production: The Apparel Industry in the Pacific Rim,* edited by Edna Bonacich, Lucie Cheng, Norma Chinchilla, Nora Hamilton, and Paul Ong, 42–62. Philadelphia: Temple University Press.

Appelbaum, Richard P., and Jeffrey Henderson. 1995. "The Hinge of History: Turbulence and Transformation in the World Economy." *Competition and Change: Journal of Global Business and Political Economy* 1 (1): 1–12.

Archibald, Linda, and Mary Crnkovich. 1995. "Intimate Outsiders: Feminist Research in a Cross-Cultural Environment." In *Changing Methods: Feminists Transforming Practice,* edited by Sandra Burt and Lorraine Code, 105–25. Peterborough, Ontario: Broadview Press.

Arrighi, Giovanni. 1994. *The Long Twentieth Century.* London: Verso.

Auyero, Javier. 1999. "From the Client's Point(s) of View: How Poor People Perceive and Evaluate Political Clientelism." *Theory and Society* 28 (2): 297–334.

———. 2002. *Poor People's Politics: Peronist Survival Networks and the Legacy of Evita.* Durham: Duke University Press.

Báez, Clara, and Ginny Taulé. "Posición socio-cultural y economica de la mujer en la Republica Dominicana." *Género y Sociedad* 1 (2).

Baud, Michiel. 1995. *Peasants and Tobacco in the Dominican Republic, 1870–1930*. Knoxville: University of Tennessee Press.

Baver, Sherrie L., and Barbara Deutsch Lynch. 2006. "The Political Ecology of Paradise." In *Beyond Sun and Sand: Caribbean Environmentalisms*, edited by Sherrie Baver and Barbara Deutsch Lynch, 3–16. New Brunswick: Rutgers University Press.

Bennett, Tony, et al., eds. 1981. *Culture, Ideology, and Social Process*. London: Open University Press.

Bergeron, Suzanne. 2001. "Political Economy Discourses of Globalization and Feminist Politics." *Signs* 26 (4): 983–1006.

Betances, Emilio. 1995. *The State and Society in the Dominican Republic*. Boulder, Colo.: Westview Press.

Bhavnani, Kum-Kum. 1988. "Empowerment and Social Research: Some Comments." *Text* 8 (1–2): 41–50.

———. 1993. "Tracing the Contours: Feminist Research and Feminist Objectivity." *Women's Studies International Forum* 16 (2): 95–104.

Bhavnani, Kum-Kum, John Foran, and Priya Kurian. 2003. "An Introduction to Women, Culture, and Development." In *Feminist Futures: Re-imagining Women, Culture, and Development*, edited by Kum-Kum Bhavnani, John Foran, and Priya Kurian, 1–22. London: Zed Books.

Blumberg, Rae Lesser. 1995. Introduction to *EnGENDERing Wealth and Well-Being: Empowerment for Global Change*, edited by Ray Lesser Blumberg, Cathy A. Rakowski, Irene Tinker, and Michael Monteón, 1–14. San Francisco: Westview Press.

———. 2001. "'We Are Family': Gender, Microenterprise, Family Work, and Well-Being in Ecuador and the Dominican Republic—with Comparative Data from Guatemala, Swaziland, and Guinea-Bissau." *History of the Family* 6 (2): 271–99.

Bonó, Pedro Francisco. 1968. *El Montero*. Santo Domingo, Dominican Republic: Julio D. Postigo e Hijos.

Boserup, Ester. 1970. *Women's Role in Economic Development*. New York: Saint Martin's Press.

Bourdieu, Pierre. 1986. "The Forms of Social Capital." In *Handbook of Theory and Research for the Sociology of Education*, edited by J. G. Richardson, 241–58. New York: Greenwood Press.

Braidotti, Rosi, Ewa Charkiewicz, Sabine Hausler, Saskia Wieringa. 1994. *Women, the Environment, and Sustainable Development: Towards a Theoretical Synthesis*. London: Zed Books.

Brea, Ramonina, and Isis Duarte. 1999. *Entre la calle y la casa: Las mujeres dominicanas y la cultura política a finales del siglo XX*. Santo Domingo, Dominican Republic: Profamilia.

Brennan, Denise. 2004. *What's Love Got to Do with It: Transnational Desires and Sex Tourism in the Dominican Republic*. Durham: Duke University Press.

Bueno, Lourdes. 1993. "Mujer y desarrollo: La experiencia de los proyectos de generación de ingresos." *Género y Sociedad* 1 (1): 21–29.

Burac, Maurice. 2006. "The Struggle for Sustainable Tourism in Martinique." In *Beyond Sun and Sand: Caribbean Environmentalisms*, edited by Sherrie Baver and Barbara Deutsch Lynch, 65–74. New Brunswick: Rutgers University Press.

Burgess, Robert. 1984. *In the Field: An Introduction to Field Research*. London: Macmillan.

Calder, Bruce J. 1984. *The Impact of Intervention: The Dominican Republic During the U.S. Occupation of 1916–1924*. Austin: University of Texas Press.

Carodoso, Fernando Enrique, and Enzo Faletto. 1971. *Dependency and Development in Latin America*. Translated by Marjory Mattingly Urquidi. Berkeley and Los Angeles: University of California Press.

Cassá, Roberto. 1992. *Historia social y economica de la Republica Dominicana*. 11th ed. Santo Domingo, Dominican Republic: Editora Alfa y Omega.

Centro de Estudios Sociales y Demográficos. 1997. *Encuesta Demográfica y de Salud 1996 (ENDESA 96)*. Calverton, Md.: Macro International.

Chua, Peter, Kum-Kum Bhavnani, and John Foran. 2000. "Women, Culture, and Development: A New Paradigm for Development Studies." *Ethnic and Racial Studies* 23 (5): 820–41.

Comaroff, John, and Jean Comaroff. 1992. *Ethnography and the Historical Imagination*. Boulder, Colo.: Westview Press.

Cordero Michel, Emilio. 2000. *La revolución haitiana y Santo Domingo*. Santo Domingo, Dominican Republic: La Universidad Abierta para Adultos, Facultad Latino Americana de Ciencias Sociales sede Santo Domingo.

Corten, Andre, and Isis Duarte. 1994. "Quinientos mil haitianos en Republica Dominicana." *Estudios Sociales* 98 (October–November): 7–36.

Dankelman, Irene, and Joan Davidson. 1988. *Women and Environment in the World: Alliances for the Future*. London: Earthscan.

Deere, Carmen Diana, and Magdalena León, eds. 1987. *Rural Women and State Policy*. Boulder, Colo.: Westview Press.

Derby, Robin, and Richard Turits. 1993. "Historias de terror y los terrores de la historia: La massacre haitiana de 1937 en la Republica Dominicana." *Estudios Sociales* 92: 65–76.

Diamond, Jared. 2005. *Collapse: How Societies Choose to Fail or Succeed*. New York: Penguin.

Dirección General de Promoción de la Mujer. 1994. *Informe Nacional (Versión Preliminar) Conferencia de las Naciones Unidas sobre la Mujer "Acción para la igualdad, el desarrollo, y la paz," Beijing, China 1995*. Santo Domingo, Dominican Republic: Secretariado Técnico de la Presidencia, Dirección General de Promoción de la Mujer.

Dore Cabral, Carlos. 1986. "El debate actual sobre la reforma agraria (notas para una propuesta de Estudio)." *Ciéncia y Sociedad* 11 (4): 460–73.

Dotzauer, Helmut. 1993. "The Political and Socio-economic Factors Causing Forest Degradation in the Dominican Republic." *Rural Development Forestry Network*. London: Overseas Development Institute.

Duany, Jorge. 1998. "Reconstructing Racial Identity: Ethnicity, Color, and Class Among Dominicans in the United States and Puerto Rico." *Latin American Perspectives* 25 (3): 147–72.

Duneier, Mitchell. 1999. *Sidewalk*. New York: Farrar, Straus and Giroux.

Escobar, Arturo. 1995. *Encountering Development: The Making and Unmaking of the Third World*. Princeton: Princeton University Press.

———. 2001. "'Culture Sits in Places': Reflections on Globalism and Subaltern Strategies of Localization." *Political Geography* 20:139–74.

Espinal, Rosario. 1995. "Economic Restructuring, Social Protest, and Democratization in the Dominican Republic." *Latin American Perspectives* 22 (3): 63–79.

Fanon, Frantz. 1967. *Black Skin, White Masks*. New York: Grove Press.

Feldman, Shelley, and Rick Welsh. 1995. "Feminist Knowledge Claims, Local Knowledge, and Gender Divisions of Agricultural Labor: Constructing a Successor Science." *Rural Sociology* 60 (1): 23–43.

Ferguson, James. 1992. *Dominican Republic: Beyond the Lighthouse*. London: Latin American Bureau.

Finlay, Barbara. 1989. *Women of Azua: Work and Family in the Rural Dominican Republic*. New York: Praeger.

Flax, Jane. 1992. "The End of Innocence." In *Feminists Theorize the Political*, edited by Judith Butler and Joan Scott, 445–63. New York: Routledge.

Flora, Cornelia, and Blas Santos. 1985. "Women in Farming Systems in Latin America." In *Women and Change in Latin America*, edited by June Nash and Helen Safa, 208–28. South Hadley, Mass.: Bergin and Garvey.

Fonow, Mary Margaret, and Judith A. Cook. 1991. *Beyond Methodology: Feminist Scholarship as Lived Research*. Bloomington: Indiana University Press.

Forgacs, David, ed. 2000. *The Antonio Gramsci Reader: Selected Writings, 1916–1935*. New York: New York University Press.

Foucault, Michel. 1984. "The Subject and Power." In *Art After Modernism: Rethinking Representation*, edited by Brian Wallis, 417–34. New York: New Museum of Contemporary Art in association with David Godine.

Franco, Franklin. 1997. *Sobre racismo y anti-haitianismo (y otros ensayos)*. Santo Domingo, Dominican Republic: Impresora Vidal.

Freeman, Carla. 2001. "Is Local : Global as Feminine : Masculine? Rethinking the Gender of Globalization." *Signs* 26 (4): 1007–38.

Furtado, Celso. 1986. "Economic Development of Latin America." In *Promise of Development: Theories of Change in Latin America*, edited by Peter F. Klarén and Thomas J. Bossert, 124–48. Boulder, Colo.: Westview Press.

Galeano, Eduardo. 1988. *Memory of Fire III: Century of the Wind*. Translated by Cedric Belfrage. New York: Pantheon Books.

———. 1993. *Las palabras andantes*. Mexico: Siglo Ventiuno Editores.

Galíndez, Jesús de. 1973. *The Era of Trujillo*. Tucson: University of Arizona Press.

García Canclini, Néstor. 1995. *Hybrid Cultures: Strategies for Entering and Leaving Modernity*. Minneapolis: University of Minnesota Press.

García-Guadilla, María Pilar. 1995. "Gender, Environment, and Empowerment in Venezuela." In *EnGENDERing Wealth and Well-Being: Empowerment for Global Change*, edited by Rae Lesser Blumberg, Cathy A. Rakowski, Irene Tinker, and Michael Monteón, 213–37. San Francisco: Westview Press.

Georges, Eugenia. 1990. *The Making of a Transnational Community: Migration, Development, and Cultural Change in the Dominican Republic*. New York: Columbia University Press.

Gereffi, Gary. 1994. "Capitalism, Development, and Global Commodity Chains." In *Capitalism and Development*, edited by Leslie Sklair, 211–31. New York: Routledge.

Gill, Lesley. 1997. "Power Lines: The Political Context of Nongovernmental Organization (NGO) Activity in Alto, Bolivia." *Journal of Latin American Anthropology* 2 (2):144–69.

González, Raymundo. 1993. "Ideología del progreso y campesinado en el siglo XIX." *Ecos* 1 (2): 25–43.

Gordon, Avery. 1997. *Ghostly Matters: Haunting and the Sociological Imagination*. Minneapolis: University of Minnesota Press.

Grasmuck, Sherrie, and Rosario Espinal. 1997. "Gender Households and Informal Entrepreneurship in the Dominican Republic." *Journal of Comparative Family Studies* 28:103–28.

————. 2001. "Market Success or Female Autonomy: Income, Ideology, and Empowerment Among Micro-entrepreneurs in the Dominican Republic." *Gender and Society* 14 (2): 231–55.

Guerrero, María Angustias. 1991. *Tras las huellas . . . La mujer dominicana en el mundo del trabajo 1900–1950.* Santo Domingo, Dominican Republic: Centro de Investigación para la Acción Femenina.

Gunder Frank, Andre. 1969. "Sociology of Development and Underdevelopment of Sociology." In *Latin America: Underdevelopment or Revolution,* edited by Andre Gunder Frank, 21–94. New York: Monthly Review Press.

Haggis, Jane. 1990. "The Feminist Research Process—Defining a Topic." In *Feminist Praxis: Research, Theory, and Epistemology in Feminist Sociology,* edited by Liz Stanley, 67–79. London: Routledge.

Hall, Stuart. 1981. "Cultural Studies: Two Paradigms." In *Culture, Ideology, and Social Process: A Reader,* edited by Tony Bennett, Graham Martin, Colin Mener, and Janet Woollacott. London: Open University Press.

————. 1992. "New Ethnicities." In *Race, Culture, and Difference,* edited by James Donald and Ali Rattansi, 252–59. London: Sage.

————. 1996. "Gramsci's Relevance for the Study of Race and Ethnicity." In *Critical Dialogues in Cultural Studies,* edited by David Morley and Kuan-Hsing Chen, 411–40. London: Routledge.

Haraway, Donna. 1988. "Situated Knowledges: The Science Question in Feminism and the Privilege of Partial Perspective." *Feminist Studies* 14 (3): 475–599.

Harcourt, Wendy. 1994. "Negotiating Positions in the Sustainable Development Debate: Situating a Feminist Perspective." In *Feminist Perspectives on Sustainable Development,* edited by Wendy Harcourt, 11–25. London: Zed Books.

Harvey, Lee. 1990. *Critical Social Research.* London: Macmillan.

Inoa, Orlando. 1999. *Azucar: Arabes, cocolos y haitianos.* Santo Domingo, Dominican Republic: Editora Cole y Facultad Latino Americana de Ciencias Sociales.

Jansen, Senaida, and Roldán Mármol. 1996. *Nosotras, las que caminamos.* Santo Domingo, Dominican Republic: Helvetas.

Jayaratne, Toby Epstein, and Abigail Stewart. 1991. "Quantitative and Qualitative Methods in the Social Sciences: Current Feminist Issues and Practical Strategies." In *Beyond Methodology: Feminist Scholarship as Lived Research,* edited by Mary Margaret Fonow and Judith A. Cook, 85–106. Bloomington: Indiana University Press.

Katz, Cindi. 1996. "The Expeditions of Conjurers: Ethnography, Power, and Pretense." In *Feminist Dilemmas in Fieldwork,* edited by Diane L. Wolf, 170–84. Boulder, Colo.: Westview Press.

Kincaid, Jamaica. 1988. *A Small Place.* New York: Farrar, Straus and Giroux.

Klarén, Peter F. 1986. "The Lost Promise: Explaining Latin American Underdevelopment." In *Promise of Development: Theories of Change in Latin America,* edited by Peter F. Klarén and Thomas J. Bossert, 3–36. Boulder, Colo.: Westview Press.

Krohn-Hansen, Christian. 1996. "Masculinity and the Political Among Dominicans: 'The Dominican Tiger.'" In *Machos, Mistresses, and Madonnas: Contesting the Power of Latin American Gender Imagery,* edited by Marit Melhuus and Kristi Anne Stolen, 108–33. New York: Verso.

Kustudia, Michael. 1997. "The Contested Cordillera: Forest Conversion and Conflict in a Dominican Watershed." Master's thesis, University of Montana.

Lambert, Jacques. 1986. "Responsibility of the Latifundios for Lags in Social Development." In *Promise of Development: Theories of Change in Latin America*, edited by Peter F. Klarén and Thomas J. Bossert, 100–106. Boulder, Colo.: Westview Press.

Lind, Amy Conger. 1992. "Power, Gender, and Development: Popular Women's Organizations and the Politics of Needs in Ecuador." In *The Making of Social Movements in Latin America: Identity, Strategy, and Democracy*, edited by Arturo Escobar and Sonia Alvarez, 134–49. Boulder, Colo.: Westview Press.

Lipset, Seymour Martin. 1986. "Values, Education, and Entrepreneurship." In *Promise of Development: Theories of Change in Latin America*, edited by Peter F. Klarén and Thomas J. Bossert, 39–75. Boulder, Colo.: Westview Press.

Lynch, Barbara Deutsch. 2006. "Seeking Agricultural Sustainability: Cuban and Dominican Strategies." In *Beyond Sun and Sand: Caribbean Environmentalisms*, edited by Sherrie Baver and Barbara Deutsch Lynch, 86–108. New Brunswick: Rutgers University Press.

Marcus, George E. 1986. "Contemporary Problems of Ethnography in the Modern World System." In *Writing Culture: The Poetics and Politics of Ethnography*, edited by James Clifford and George Marcus, 165–93. Berkeley and Los Angeles: University of California Press.

———. 1998. *Ethnography Through Thick and Thin*. Princeton: Princeton University Press.

Mariñez, Pablo. 1984. *Resistencia campesina, imperialismo y reforma agraria en República Dominicana (1899–1978)*. Santo Domingo, Dominican Republic: Centro de Planificación y Acción Ecuménica.

———. 1993. *Agroindustria, estado y clases sociales en la era de Trujillo (1935–1960)*. Santo Domingo, Dominican Republic: Fundación Cultural Dominicana.

Martínez, Eleuterio. 1990. *Los bosques dominicanos*. Santo Domingo, Dominican Republic: Editora Horizontes de América.

Martínez-Vergne, Teresita. 2005. *Nation and Citizen in the Dominican Republic, 1880–1916*. Chapel Hill: University of North Carolina Press.

Matsumoto, Valerie. 1996. "Reflections on Oral History: Research in a Japanese American Community." In *Feminist Dilemmas in Fieldwork*, edited by Diane L. Wolf, 160–69. Boulder, Colo.: Westview Press.

Menchú, Rigoberta. 1984. *I, Rigoberta Menchú: An Indian Woman in Guatemala*. Edited by Elisabeth Burgos-Debray. Translated by Ann Wright. New York: Verso.

Mernissi, Fatima. 1989. *Doing Daily Battle: Interviews with Moroccan Women*. Translated by Mary Jo Lakeland. New Brunswick: Rutgers University Press.

Miller, Marian A. L. 2006. "Paradise Sold, Paradise Lost: Jamaica's Environment and Culture in the Tourism Marketplace." In *Beyond Sun and Sand: Caribbean Environmentalisms*, edited by Sherrie Baver and Barbara Deutsch Lynch, 35–44. New Brunswick: Rutgers University Press.

Mohanty, Chandra Talpade. 1991. "Under Western Eyes: Feminist Scholarship and Colonial Discourses." In *Third World Women and the Politics of Feminism*, edited by Chandra Talpade Mohanty, Ann Russo, and Lourdes Torres. Bloomington: Indiana University Press.

Momsen, Janet Henshall. 1993. Introduction to *Women and Change in the Caribbean*, edited by Janet Momsen, 1–11. Bloomington: Indiana University Press.

Moreno, José A. 1986. "Economic Crisis in the Caribbean: From Traditional to Modern Dependency: The Case of the Dominican Republic." Translated by Jerry Decker. *Contemporary Marxism* 14:97–114.

Moya Pons, Frank. 1997. *Manual de Historia Dominicana.* 11th ed. Santo Domingo, Dominican Republic: Caribbean.

Mummert, Gail. 1996. "Industrialization and Changing Gender Roles in Rural Michoacán, Mexico." In *Emergences: Women's Struggles for Livelihood in Latin America,* edited by John Friedmann, Rebecca Abers, and Lilian Autler. Los Angeles: University of California, Los Angeles, Latin American Center.

Munck, Ronaldo, and Denis O'Hearn, eds. 1999. *Critical Development Theory: Contributions to a New Paradigm.* London: Zed Books.

Muppidi, Himadeep. 2004. *The Politics of the Global.* Minneapolis: University of Minnesota Press.

Narayan, Uma. 2000. "Essence of Culture and a Sense of History: A Feminist Critique of Cultural Essentialism." In *Decentering the Center: Philosophy for a Multicultural, Postcolonial, and Feminist World,* edited by Uma Narayan and Sandra Harding, 80–100. Bloomington: Indiana University Press.

Omi, Michael, and Howard Winant. 1994. *Racial Formation in the United States from the 1960s to the 1990s.* 2d ed. New York: Routledge.

Ong, Aihwa. 1987. *Spirits of Resistance and Capitalist Discipline: Factory Women in Malaysia.* Albany: State University of New York Press.

———. 1988. "Colonialism and Modernity: Feminist Re-Presentations of Non-Western Societies." *Inscriptions* 3 (4): 79–93.

Ortuño, Francisco. 1987. *Estudio de la legislación e instituciones forestales en la República Dominicana.* Santo Domingo, Dominican Republic: Banco Interamericano de Desarrollo.

Paiewonsky, Margarita. 1993. "Imagen de la mujer en los textos de historia dominicana." *Género y Sociedad* 1 (1): 30–59.

Parpart, Jane. 1995. "Post-modernism, Gender, and Development." In *Power of Development,* edited by Jonathan Crush, 253–65. New York: Routledge.

Parpart, Jane L., and Marianne H. Marchant. 1995. "Exploding the Canon: An Introduction/Conclusion." In *Feminism, Postmodernism, Development,* edited by Jane L. Parpart and Marianne H. Marchand. New York: Routledge.

Pau, Francis, et al. 1987. *La Mujer Rural Dominicana.* Santo Domingo, Dominican Republic: Centro de Investigación para la Acción Femenina.

Paulino, Edward. 2005. "Erasing the Kreyol from the Margins of the Dominican Republic: The Pre- and Post-nationalization Project of the Border, 1930–1935." *Wadabagei: A Journal of the Caribbean and Its Diaspora* 8 (2): 35–71.

Peluso, Nancy Lee. 1995. "Whose Woods Are These? Counter-mapping Forest Territories in Kalimantan, Indonesia." *Antipode* 27 (4): 383–406.

Pérez Rancier, Juan B. 1972. *Geografía y sociedad.* Santo Domingo, Dominican Republic: Editora del Caribe.

Pigg, Stacey Leigh. 2005. "Globalizing the Facts of Life." In *Sex and Development: Science, Sexuality, and Morality in Global Perspective,* edited by Vincanne Adams and Stacey Leigh Pigg, 39–65. Durham: Duke University Press.

Piñeda, Magaly. 1990. ". . . *La vida mía no es fácil": La otra cara de la zona franca.* Santo Domingo, Dominican Republic: Centro de Investigación para la Acción Femenina.

Quiroga, Hiram, Santiago Quevedo, and Eduardo Chiriboga. 1995. *Hacia el cambio mediante la autogestión comunitaria.* Quito: Imprenta Cotopaxi.

Rakowski, Cathy A. 1995. "Conclusion: Engendering Wealth and Well-Being—Lessons Learned." In *EnGENDERing Wealth and Well-Being: Empowerment for Global*

Change, edited by Rae Lesser Blumberg, Cathy A. Rakowski, Irene Tinker, and Michael Monteón, 213–37. San Francisco: Westview Press.

Rathgeber, Eva. 1990. "WID, WAD, GAD: Trends in Research and Practice." *Journal of Developing Areas* 24:489–502.

Rawneema, Majid, and Victoria Bawtree, eds. 1997. *The Post-development Reader.* London: Zed Books.

Raynolds, Laura, T. 2001. "New Plantations, New Workers: Gender and Production in Politics in the Dominican Republic." *Gender and Society* 15 (1): 7–28.

———. 2002. "Wages for Wives: Renegotiating Gender and Production Relations in Contract Farming in the Dominican Republic." *World Development* 30 (5): 783–98.

Rocheleau, Dianne. 2005. "Cultures of Peace: Women in the Rural Federation of Zambrana-Chacuey." *Development* 48 (3): 93–100.

Rocheleau, Dianne, and Laurie Ross. 1995. "Trees as Tools, Trees as Text: Struggles over Resources in Zambrana-Chacuey, Dominican Republic." *Antipode* 27 (4): 407–28.

Rocheleau, Dianne, et al. 1996. "From Forest Gardens to Tree Farms." In *Feminist Political Ecology: Global Issues and Local Experiences,* edited by Diane Rocheleau, Barbara Thomas-Slayter, and Esther Wangari, 224–50. New York: Routledge.

Roorda, Eric Paul. 1998. *The Good Neighbor Policy and the Trujillo Regime in the Dominican Republic, 1930–1945.* Durham: Duke University Press.

Rosario, Pedro Juan del. 1989. "Economía rural de la Republica Dominicana: Una nueva visión de los problemas agrarios." *Eme Eme* 15 (83): 17–76.

Rostow, W. W. 1960. *The Stages of Economic Growth: A Non-Communist Manifesto.* Cambridge: Cambridge University Press.

Safa, Helen I. 1995a. "Gender Implications of Export-Led Industrialization in the Caribbean Basin." In *EnGENDERing Wealth and Well-Being: Empowerment for Global Change,* edited by Rae Lesser Blumberg, Cathy A. Rakowski, Irene Tinker, and Michael Monteón, 89–112. San Francisco: Westview Press.

———. 1995b. *The Myth of the Male Breadwinner: Women and Industrialization in the Caribbean.* San Francisco: Westview Press.

———. 1998. "Introduction: Race and National Identity in the Americas." *Latin American Perspectives* 25 (3): 3–20.

Said, Edward. 1994. *Culture and Imperialism.* New York: Vintage Books.

Saldaña-Portillo, María Josefina. 2003. *The Revolutionary Imagination in the Americas and the Age of Development.* Durham: Duke University Press.

Salzinger, Leslie. 2003. *Genders in Production: Making Workers in Mexico's Global Factories.* Berkeley and Los Angeles: University of California Press.

Sanchez, Nestor. 1994. "Community Development and the Role of the NGOs: A New Perspective for Latin America in the 1990s." *Community Development Journal* 29 (4): 307–19.

San Miguel, Pedro L. 1995. "Peasant Resistance to State Demands in the Cibao During U.S. Occupation." *Latin American Perspectives* 22 (3): 41–62.

———. 2005. *The Imagined Island: History, Identity, and Utopia in Hispaniola.* Translated by Jane Ramírez. Chapel Hill: University of North Carolina Press.

Scholz, Claudia. 2002. "Cultivating Social Capital for Development." Paper presented at the Annual Meeting of the Rural Sociology Society, August 14–18, in Chicago, Illinois.

Scott, Catherine. 1995. *Gender and Development: Rethinking Modernization and Dependency Theory.* Boulder, Colo.: Lynne Rienner.

Sen, Gita, and Karen Grown. 1987. *Development, Crisis, and Alternative Visions*. New York: Monthly Review Press.

Serulle Ramia, José. 1997. *La agropecuaria dominicana*. Santo Domingo, Dominican Republic: Ediciones Fundación Ciencia y Arte.

Shiva, Vandana. 1991. *The Violence of the Green Revolution*. London: Zed Books.

Silvert, Kalman H. 1986. "The Politics of Social and Economic Change in Latin America." In *Promise of Development: Theories of Change in Latin America*, edited by Peter F. Klarén and Thomas J. Bossert, 76–87. Boulder, Colo.: Westview Press.

Stanley, Liz, and Sue Wise. 1990. "Method, Methodology, and Epistemology in Feminist Research Processes." In *Feminist Praxis: Research, Theory, and Epistemology in Feminist Sociology*, edited by Liz Stanley, 20–62. London: Routledge.

Suárez Findlay, Eileen J. 1999. *Imposing Decency: The Politics of Sexuality and Race in Puerto Rico, 1870–1920*. Durham: Duke University Press.

Thomas, Jim. 1993. *Doing Critical Ethnography*. Newbury Park, Calif.: Sage.

Thomas-Slayter, Barbara, and Dianne Rocheleau, eds. 1995. *Gender, Environment, and Development in Kenya: A Grassroots Perspective*. Boulder, Colo.: Lynne Rienner.

Torres-Saillant, Silvio. 1998. "The Tribulations of Blackness: Stages in Dominican Racial Identity." *Latin American Perspectives* 25 (3): 126–46.

Tsing, Anna Lowenhaupt. 1993. *In the Realm of the Diamond Queen*. Princeton: Princeton University Press.

———. 2005. *Friction: An Ethnography of Global Connection*. Princeton: Princeton University Press.

Turits, Richard Lee. 1997. "The Foundations of Despotism: Peasants, Property, and the Trujillo Regime (1930–1961)." Ph.D. diss., University of Chicago.

———. 2003. *Foundations of Despotism: Peasants, the Trujillo Regime, and Modernity in Dominican History*. Stanford, Calif.: Stanford University Press.

Twine, France Winddance. 1998. *Racism in a Racial Democracy: The Maintenance of White Supremacy in Brazil*. New Brunswick: Rutgers University Press.

Vandegrift, Darcie. 1998. "Reading Resistance to Imagine Change: Bribri Women and International Development in Costa Rica."

Vargas-Lundius, Rosemary. 1992. *Peasants in Distress: Poverty and Unemployment in the Dominican Republic*. Boulder, Colo.: Westview Press.

Vergara, Ricardo. 1994. "NGOs: Help or Hindrance for Community Development in Latin America." *Community Development Journal* 29 (4): 322–28.

Wallerstein, Immanuel. 1974. *The Modern World-System*. New York: Academic Press.

Weyland, Karin. 2005. "Género y transnacionalismo en la encrucijada de agendas locales y globales: De Nueva York a Villa Mella." In *Miradas desencadenantes: Los Estudios de Género en la República Dominicana al inicio del Tercer Milenio*, edited by Ginetta Candelario, 209–30. Santo Domingo, Dominican Republic: Instituto Tecnológico.

Williams, Raymond. 1977. *Marxism and Literature*. Oxford: Oxford University Press.

———. 1981. *The Sociology of Culture*. Chicago: University of Chicago Press.

Wolf, Diane L. 1996. "Situating Feminist Dilemmas in Fieldwork." In *Feminist Dilemmas in Fieldwork*, edited by Diane L. Wolf, 1–54. Boulder, Colo.: Westview Press.

Wood, Cynthia. 2001. "Authorizing Gender and Development: 'Third World Women,' Native Informants, and Speaking Nearby." *Nepantla: Views from South* 2 (3): 429–47.

Wright, Melissa. 1999. "The Dialectics of Still Life: Murder, Women, and Maquiladoras." *Public Culture* 11 (3): 453–74.

INDEX